Carried Within Me

Carried Within Me

Echoes of Infant Loss
from Bereaved Parents

By Joann Cantrell

Lighthouse Point Press

Pittsburgh, Pennsylvania

Carried Within Me:
Echoes of Infant Loss
from Bereaved Parents
Joann Cantrell

Published by Lighthouse Point Press
Pittsburgh, Pennsylvania

www.lighthousepointpress.com

https://joanncantrell.wordpress.com

ISBN: **978-0-9792998-4-1**

Printed in the United States of America

DEDICATION

For Kevin and Art.
In honor of their brief lives.
April 2, 1990

CONTENTS

INTRODUCTION

This book is a collection of narratives from contributors who responded to a feature I did for the *Pittsburgh Post-Gazette* that was published on International Bereaved Mother's Day, May 7, 2017. Telling my story, I welcomed women to contact me whose infants were stillborn or died shortly after birth.

At first, I heard only from mothers who had experienced this loss recently, but then I started to hear from many who lost infants long ago. Despite the span of decades, their grief was the same, as was the expressions of longing for their child. Each mother felt isolated until hearing of others who had also suffered the loss of their baby, and there was comfort and unity in that understanding.

I lost infant twin sons twenty-nine years ago and know firsthand that it is a loss that one never gets over. Our boys arrived too soon, after I had carried them nearly six months. Ironically, it was the same time of year that the crocuses were popping up from under the snow, making their comeback after a harsh winter.

Like the flowers, my babies were early in blooming, yet they lacked the strength to survive.

Two days after their births, my husband and I buried our babies together in one tiny coffin in a cemetery near our home. It also happened to be our wedding anniversary, a day intended for celebration rather than sorrow. I clearly remember my heart feeling as frozen as the snow-covered ground.

Even the undertaker wept as he placed their coffin near the grave, and I felt that they might as well have buried me, too. My emotions were on a wild roller coaster after the unexpected labor and delivery of our twins, followed by their deaths and making arrangements for a funeral and burial. In the following weeks, Mother's Day was erased from that year's calendar.

The worst part of the grieving was that people felt uncomfortable with the loss. It was confusing to acknowledge a birth while expressing sympathy over a death. My grief was expected to be temporary, as there was never time to know the babies. Kevin and Art were our fourth and fifth children. Well-meaning relatives and friends attempted consolation with the inappropriate reminder that at least we had three others. Support was hard to find.

At first, I questioned if I should open the door again and write about this. Then I spoke with Stephanie, the first bereaved mother I interviewed.

I met her on a rainy day in a coffee shop, and she was crying as hard as it was raining. When we planned to meet, I didn't know that she had just lost her baby girl, Scarlett, four weeks earlier.

Stephanie desperately needed support and didn't know where to go. She was still in a state of shock, right in the eye of the storm of grief.

That confirmed my instincts for the concept of this book. I was so far down the road on my own personal journey of grief that I had a different perspective. I had gained a deep connection to other mothers who had gone through the same loss and realized that perhaps the resilience and sense of survival they displayed might help to encourage the same in others.

The common loss transcends time and opens the heart, affirming the need to discuss and validating the need to be understood and listened to, especially by those who were felt forced to forget and move on in silence.

In the interviews, many of the participants opened up about a part of their lives they had never shared before. Many began to weep despite the decades that had passed and the recent bereaved mothers displayed the raw emotion in their stories.

It was too soon for Stephanie, but I knew that she and the countless other newly bereaved mothers that I met were the ones I would be writing for, hoping to give an empathetic message of understanding and the possibility of hope.

As a writer, I am now hoping to give back and offer the support and comfort I received all those years ago with this collection of narratives from those who have also experienced such a heartbreaking loss.

My twin sons, Kevin and Art, were born and died on April 2, 1990, a time when infant loss was not discussed and young mothers suffered in silence. Had it not been for a sympathetic staff at the hospital who pointed me in the direction of a local support group, I don't know how I would have managed my grief. The organization known as SHARE—Self-Help and Recovery Exchange—made an early effort to bring bereaved parents together to share their experiences.

The stories and essays in this book are heartfelt and shared for newly bereaved mothers, fathers and family members as a way to relate and connect to a supporting community of those who have walked the same journey, letting them know they're not alone.

Each essay and letter communicates the individual way each parent coped after the loss of their baby. At the core of each story is that parent's personal path of resilience through hardship, despair and hopelessness. In this book, bereaved parents relate how they have found ways to continue to live with new meaning. By reading these shared experiences of infant loss, newly bereaved parents can begin to muster hope that just like the flowering crocuses, they, too, will survive the harshest conditions and know that they are not alone in their struggle.

CHAPTER 1

DISBELIEF AND EMPTINESS

I was in a state of disbelief when my twin baby boys were born on a cold April morning and died slightly more than thirty minutes later. I was thirty years old and had endured three previous textbook pregnancies that delivered three healthy children. The traumatic births of my fourth and fifth babies were unthinkable.

Later in the evening, from my dark and solitary hospital room, when the nurse asked me if I needed anything, I asked if she could bring me a pen and paper. The urge to write was so strong.

I was given a few sheets of paper that had postpartum exercises printed on them and as the nurse turned them over to the blank side, I remember her saying, "Here you go honey, you can write on this."

The pages contained eight diagrams on abdominal exercises for sit-ups, toning, and pelvic tilts. I stared at the instructions and thought of the irony—there was information on how to help my body, yet no instructions on how to mentally recover if your babies had died.

I was lost without knowing what to do.

And so, I scribbled words in the late hours of that awful day that my twin boys were born and died. My handwriting was unrecognizable—the downhill slant of my penmanship was indicative of my emotions spiraling out of control.

So empty—such an empty, lonely feeling.
So much sadness.
I lost my twin boys this morning. They lived and died within minutes.
So tiny, they looked like little birds. They were so helpless.
Such a quiet, empty, lonely feeling. No more life inside of me.

REMEMBERING ELLA GRACE,
as told by her mother, Jaime

"I remember the feeling of wanting to be a mom so badly, but then accepting that I was a mom. Even though everyone didn't know that I was a mom because I wasn't holding a baby, I felt like a mother. Today, any painful experience that my husband and I have gone through with life, marriage, and raising children has always paled in comparison to losing Ella."

 Jaime and Chad had been married for two years when their daughter, Ella Grace was born and died on January 14, 2008. The couple had found out they were expecting in August 2007 and were excited for their first pregnancy.

Jaime's older sister was pregnant at the time with her second child. She was due in March, and Jaime was due in May. Jaime and Chad didn't want to find out the gender of the baby but had an ultrasound at eighteen weeks and everything looked great.

At twenty-two weeks, when Jaime experienced some spotting, she knew, as a nurse, that it was sometimes normal, but still felt like something wasn't right. She had a doctor's appointment scheduled the next day, and it was also her husband's birthday, so they had planned to go to the appointment and then out to lunch.

Jaime told her obstetrician about the spotting. She had known him for a few years since she was a nurse in the postpartum unit at Magee Women's Hospital in Pittsburgh for almost four years. He could sense her concern and checked her cervix to make sure she wasn't dilated.

"I could tell by the look on his face when he was checking me that it wasn't good news. I was three centimeters dilated, and he could feel the amniotic sac was bulging through," Jaime recalls. "I knew right away from a medical perspective that was not a good outcome at twenty-two weeks."

She was immediately admitted to the hospital where she was employed, and the doctors and her coworkers were extremely supportive and hopeful. Friends and family prayed and thought that she could hang on for a few more weeks. She was hopeful that if she could make it to twenty-eight weeks, the baby would be alright.

"My sister had gone into pre-term labor with my niece at twenty-eight weeks and remained in the hospital until thirty-six weeks when she delivered. I know my family was praying that I could do the same. After two days in the hospital, I wanted to be at home. I was released, but under the orders to remain on bedrest. I was also taking medication to try to stop the labor, but the doctors couldn't promise it would work. I had what they called 'painless dilation,' because I didn't feel any contractions."

The day after Jaime was released, she started to feel cramping. At this time, she knew that she was going to deliver the baby. She called the doctor at eleven p.m. and returned to the hospital with her husband. Shortly, her mother met them there, and Jaime was in labor all night. Her father and in-laws arrived in time for the baby's arrival, and Jaime delivered early in the morning.

More than a decade has passed, but Jaime can still remember every detail.

"I remember just feeling numb. We found out the baby was a girl, and everyone got to hold her. The NICU (Neonatal Intensive Care Unit) doctors came to evaluate her because she still had a heartbeat and was taking a few gasps of breath. The doctor talked to my husband and me about how she was too early to survive outside of the womb and, of course, being an OB (Obstetrics) nurse, I knew the reality of the situation. Our minister was able to come to the hospital to perform a baptism, and I just remember holding her, not wanting to let her go. As a nurse, I had seen extremely premature infants and stillborn infants, so I wasn't surprised at how she looked. She weighed one pound, four ounces.

"We had decided on the name 'Ella Grace' for a girl. 'Ella' was my great-grandmother's name, and I loved the way it sounded with 'Grace.' We still wanted to use that name for her since that is what we had picked out. I knew my grandpa would appreciate us naming her after his mother. My grandpa was a minister and had actually performed our wedding ceremony years before. It had special meaning, and I couldn't think of anything more appropriate."

A few years prior, while Jaime was finishing nursing school, she was present for the delivery of a stillborn infant. She recalled her preceptor showing her how to deal with the family and how to delicately handle the infant. She specifically remembered washing the infant and thinking how she couldn't imagine how this poor mother could cope with the circumstance of losing her child. Now, it was so surreal thinking that she was that mother, and people were thinking that about her.

"I realized that you never know how you will handle something until it happens to you," Jaime said. "We were able to spend time with her and got some pictures. The nurses washed her and dressed her in clothes that volunteers had knitted. Many of my close coworkers and doctors I worked with came to see us. I only stayed in the hospital overnight to recover, and my manager told me to take as much time as I needed off work."

In the days following, a memorial service for Ella Grace was planned. Jaime found a perfect-size dress for Ella to be buried in from a doll that her grandmother had given her as a child. Her grandmother offered a burial plot that she had purchased many years ago between Jaime's great-grandparents and uncles. Her brother surprised Jaime and Chad by flying in from out of town to be at the memorial.

The heartbreaking memories resurface easily for the bereaved young mother.

"I remember my milk had come in, and I was still in some physical pain from the delivery. It was an extremely emotional day, but I made it through. My mom had written a poem and read it at the service. I just remember personally believing that this was all happening for a reason. No one ever said that to me. Everyone was extremely supportive and kind. My sister took it very hard because she already had a daughter and was pregnant at the time. I know she felt bad that it was happening to me."

Two of Jaime's close friends and coworkers were also pregnant at the time, and she could tell everyone avoided talking about their pregnancies in front of her as time went by, even though she felt that she was coping well and could talk about it pretty easily. It helped that she worked at Magee Women's Hospital and could talk about it with coworkers. They knew a lot about it and weren't uncomfortable talking about the loss. A friend of Jaime's cousin had a stillborn a couple months prior, so she reached out to Jaime to talk about the loss of a child.

Jaime never went to therapy or a support group and, instead, felt like talking to her husband, her mom, sister, and friends, which became therapy for her. She only took three weeks off work because she was bored at home since there were no other children. She recalls being fine one minute and then crying the next minute.

"Sometimes it was a song on the radio that would make me cry. Sometimes I would wake up in the middle of the night and start crying. Through it all, my husband was very supportive."

As a nurse, Jaime knew that men cope differently than women, and she accepted the fact that Chad dealt with his emotions differently. They had been together since they were sixteen years old. Now, at twenty-six years old, she felt so comfortable with her husband that she could tell him anything. He understood that she needed to talk about the loss, even though he generally held his emotions in.

"For any couple, the main difference for a man and woman is that the mother felt her baby move inside," Jaime explained. "From the very beginning, I felt like a mom. I think it's harder for the father to feel that connection. But it was so special that Chad was able to hold Ella, because I think he had some connection then. I remember the feeling of wanting to be a mom so badly, but then accepting that I *was* a mom. Even though everyone didn't know that I was a mom because I wasn't holding a baby, I *felt like a mother.*"

As she grieved, Jaime received so many cards and notes from friends, family, and coworkers. Some people shared experiences they had that she never knew about. She found comfort and healing reading others' stories and prayers.

Her doctor was worried about her returning to work, considering what she did for a living, knowing it would be a difficult transition, but Jaime felt like she had to face her fears and return. She had worked with these people for four years, and they knew her situation and were supportive. She also had enjoyed being a postpartum nurse and had loved babies ever since she was little. Her mom told her that she always talked about how she wanted to be a baby nurse, and now, especially after the tragedy of losing Ella, Jaime didn't want to give it all up. She still believed that it happened for a reason, and God was teaching her.

"I'm not going to lie. It was extremely difficult. I cried a lot on the way to work, at work, and on the way home. Our unit was completely separate from labor and delivery, and I couldn't bring myself to even walk through that area because it brought up so many memories. My coworkers made sure everyone knew about what had happened to me so they would avoid uncomfortable conversations, yet I still always worried about how I would react if someone asked me. I had good days and bad days. I remember feeling numb a lot, too, like I was going through the motions.

"Later, when my sister had her baby, I wanted to be in the delivery room with her. Strangely, it helped me cope. My sister ended up having a girl also, and I wished so badly that our girls could have been together. In my heart, I knew that there had to be a reason."

Jaime was advised by her doctors that she should wait at least six months before getting pregnant again. She had testing done to make sure nothing was wrong with her that would prevent her from carrying a pregnancy to term. It was determined from her placenta that an infection may have been in her uterus and caused the early delivery. Doctors were hopeful that with close monitoring and weekly progesterone shots during the next pregnancy, Jaime would be able to carry a child full-term.

After what felt like the longest six months of her life, Jaime and Chad started trying right away, and she became pregnant in August, a year since she had found out she was pregnant with Ella. Her emotions ran wild—excitement and nervousness, as well. But Jaime knew that she needed to stay calm for her baby.

During the pregnancy, she met a neighbor down the street who was also expecting, and they would walk their dogs together. Jaime learned that she had suffered three miscarriages over a few years. The two women connected and found comfort and therapy talking to each other about their feelings. To this day, they are still very close friends and each have two girls that have grown up together. The friends have helped each other heal through the different stages of parenthood.

Jaime's second pregnancy went well, but still, she was always thinking about Ella. The holidays were hard the way they are when someone loses a loved one, and she was saddened by the fact that it would have been Ella's first Christmas. The one-year anniversary was difficult as well, but it felt easier to talk about Ella without completely breaking down. Jaime and Chad remembered Ella by going to her gravesite and now continue to do so each year on her birthday.

More than a year passed, and Jaime's life changed again.

"We had a beautiful baby girl in May. Mia was a month early, but really healthy, and I was thrilled to have another girl. I never felt like she would take the place of Ella, but I thought it might lessen the pain. I was so happy, but at the same time, I would have moments when I would cry. I know a lot about post-partum depression from my job, and I definitely experienced some of it for myself. My sadness came from the guilt that Mia didn't have her sister. I made it through by having the support of my mom, sister, and friends."

Another pregnancy soon followed and another beautiful girl, named Lyla, was born just short of Mia's second birthday. Jaime experienced the same feelings after having Lyla as she did with Mia. She always thought about how she would have had these three girls, and always thought she wanted three children.

"In my mind, I have had my three children. Unfortunately, one is no longer with us, but it doesn't mean she doesn't exist. I realized through more healing that I had to be grateful for the ones I have. I had gone through so much in the past couple of years and I needed to be healthy and happy for my girls."

For Jaime, it has been helpful to be completely honest with her girls. Over the years, she has taken them to Ella's grave and has explained to them about their sister.

"They know there was a baby before them, that she was born too early, and couldn't make it. They know she is in heaven and is their guardian angel. They feel comfort in the fact that they have a sister who looks over them. It probably made it easier for me to talk to them because of my profession. I think it's important for them to know so they don't feel like I was hiding something from them. We talk about it quite often, and they are alright with it."

Jaime received a letter from a coworker right after Ella was born, telling that she had a similar situation about twenty-five years before. She said that the day-to-day sadness gets easier, but it will be a part of you for the rest of your life. Now that it has been over a decade, Jaime realizes that this is true.

"I don't cry every day or week, or even every month. Certain things will trigger emotions or memories. For the most part, I just find comfort in the fact that Ella didn't suffer, and she looks over us every single day. There have been a handful of times over the years at work where I will cry or feel sad. I have shared my story with my coworkers who didn't work there at the time, to give them some perspective of how certain mothers may feel, and I have even shared my story with some mothers who I have taken care of. It's still hard some days, but I really want to help other women who are suffering. The grieving process is different for every woman. I had tons of support, and I never felt alone. I have seen through my work how many women experience loss.

"One of my biggest supporters through the loss and having my children, was a pediatrician I knew through work. He came to see me when I was in the hospital with Ella and showed so much empathy for what I had to go through. I ended up taking my girls to him, and he always asked me how I was feeling, too. He has always cared so much about my girls and was always there to listen. I still remember one of the OB doctors telling my husband and me afterwards how he hoped it was the worst thing we had to go through in our lives. To this day, it is the hardest thing, but I can't even begin to express how it has changed my life. It hasn't been all negative—it has just put a lot of things we have gone through into perspective."

"To me, there is nothing harder than burying a child, no matter how old you or your child is. My grandmother buried two children that were adults when they passed away. I think as a mother, you just always feel like you should die before your children. I feel that way about my loss, too. Even though I never got to see Ella grow up, it just makes me sad that she isn't with us. Any painful experience that my husband and I have gone through with life, marriage, and raising children has always paled in comparison to losing Ella. It has brought us closer together as a couple and made us more mature. I have met many women over the years who have lost an infant and have gone on to have other children. Many have healed or are still healing, and many have helped others heal.

"The most important lesson I have learned is that you don't know how you are going to feel or react to a loss until you have been through it. Sometimes, people are quick to judge others and how they are coping, but it's different for everyone and you can't always tell how people are going to react or grieve. It's just important to be there to listen if they need to talk.

"I found a lot of comfort in the Serenity Prayer and placed it on the back of Ella's prayer card at her memorial service. It always helps me cope with sad things I deal with at work and in life:

"God, grant me the serenity to accept the things I cannot change, the courage to change the things I can, and the wisdom to know the difference."

REMEMBERING AMELIA MARIE,
as told by her mother, Joyce

"My grandmother lost multiple children, but she passed away years before I was able to discuss this with her. It was interesting to see how many people came forward after my loss, however, and shared theirs with me. It was a true testament that losses are not typically discussed. I recall this being such an odd dynamic to the experience, when it was so important to me to talk about my child with others."

For Joyce, the journey of grief has been slow, coming now in doses rather than as a constant. She has learned what will trigger difficult times for her, and now that nearly six years have passed, she can candidly share the story of her firstborn daughter Amelia in a poignant conversation that warms her heart to remember:

Our daughter's name is Amelia Marie, and she was born on October 26, 2012. Amelia was our first child, and I was thirty-nine years old when she was delivered. I was nervous during the pregnancy because of my age, made worse by the fact that I had an anterior placenta and could only feel kicking once in a while. Due to my age and a couple of odd tests, I had more frequent doctor visits and testing. Amelia was breech for many weeks at the end of the pregnancy, so they scheduled a C-section (Caesarean) delivery at thirty-nine weeks.

At the last scheduled doctor's visit before delivery, there was no heartbeat. I was alone for the appointment because my husband was in Florida for a conference. I was induced with my family by my side, and my husband flew home in time for her breech delivery, which occurred thirty-six hours later. Several weeks before my loss my mother gave me a slip of paper with a suggested baby name. It said Amelia—Little Angel. We knew when she was in our arms that this was the name she was meant to have. Amelia was absolutely beautiful and perfect. She was small, six pounds. The family that was at the hospital was able to hold her. I was able to visit with her the next day as well.

Testing confirmed that the cause of death was a hemorrhage in the placenta. The high test result also indicated that the hemorrhage occurred shortly before the appointment. Hemorrhages of this type are usually caused by a trauma (car accident, fall, etc.), which did not occur in my case, so the cause remains unknown. I also experienced a very early miscarriage a couple years later. I was able to process this loss better because I just felt that there was something unsustainable about that life, whereas my other baby was full term and would likely still be here if she were delivered earlier. I do feel guilty at times about the miscarriage, because I could not give that child as much attention as Amelia.

In the first days and months after losing Amelia, I was initially numb. I was very angry at God, very angry at friends and family members' reactions to the loss. I wasted a lot of effort asking the unanswerable question of 'why' and looking for the justice in the loss. I felt guilty, as though there was something I should have been able to do to prevent her death. I lacked purpose and lost my identity, since I was gearing up to be a mother, but could not go through those motions. Physically, I felt great, which made me angry that I delivered a baby but had no pain while my daughter did not survive. My husband forced me off the couch (he called me on it after only one day, and that was very valuable). I emailed everyone I could think of, and this

13

communication made me feel less alone. I joined support groups. I went back to work. These actions were very helpful to me. I was still deep in grief, but I was living life.

I did have a supportive husband, family, and a few friends. However, at the time, I was not open to receiving support from anyone that did not have a similar experience. I remember struggling for support and the sense of coming up empty. That feeling was just overwhelming at first. I remember coming home from the hospital on the first night, and my husband went to bed. I was in a panic because I was completely alone and I truly didn't know if I could get through the night. One support group had a twenty-four-hour number, and I called it that night. The contact told me that she had lost a baby, and I immediately felt less alone. She visited me at home the next day, and that appointment was so valuable. I attended two support groups, both peer support, which fit my need at the time.

The peer support I received, both from groups and individuals, was the most effective for me because they had the credentials I needed before opening up and listening to them. Because I saw that these people were able to get through the experience, I gained the confidence that I could too.

I had met my husband at work, and we were friends for years before dating. He used to say that he knew I loved him because he was the only person that I ever talked to. However, after my loss, I remember talking to anyone who would listen to me about my daughter. I reached out to people I barely knew, all in an effort to feel less alone. It was comforting and amazing how many other people experienced something similar. Prior to my own loss, I did not know anyone who experienced a loss while I knew them. My grandmother lost multiple children, but she passed away years before, so I was not able to discuss this with her. It was interesting to see how many people came forward after my loss, however, and shared theirs with me. They wanted to talk about their babies, though losses were not typically discussed. I recall this being such an odd dynamic to the experience, when it was so important to me to talk about my child with others. I felt that there was no acceptable outlet for talking about my child other than in support groups.

What may have helped me more at the time, was if someone would have asked me about Amelia. I would have loved for someone to say, "Do you have any pictures? I'd love to see your baby." I did not want anyone to fix me or the situation. I did not want anyone's philosophy or faith testimony. I just wanted acknowledgement that I was a mom and that my daughter was beautiful and perfect. I have immediate family members who still have never looked at those pictures.

An interesting side note—at work, my picture of Amelia was my screensaver. After my loss, people used to look all around my office to avoid looking at her picture. However, after delivering Laura, people looked at that same screensaver of Amelia and would compliment me on my beautiful daughter, which they obviously thought was Laura. I used to love getting these secret compliments for Amelia, who never got her fair share. It was a testament to how perfect she is in that picture—that people needed the context to know something was wrong. Today, though Amelia would have been older, my desire remains the same. I like being asked about her, for her to be remembered, and for her to be included as part of my family.

Amelia was my first child. In addition to the loss was also the fear that I would never be a mother due to my age.

The statistics available to older moms and the way you are treated by OB-GYNs (Obstetric Gynecologists) did not help this matter. This led me to feel a lack of purpose, which was at times as difficult as the loss itself. I do have two beautiful daughters now, Laura and Liliana (delivered at forty and forty-one). I changed doctors, and Magee High Risk group was amazing during these stressful pregnancies. When Laura was born, I was amazed by how much she looked like Amelia. I consider this to be a gift, and often, when I look at Laura, I feel close to seeing how Amelia would look as she got older. Laura was born one year, one month, and one day after Amelia.

My grief comes in doses now. Days and weeks can go by without issue, but then something unexpected will trigger a cry session. Often, these come whenever I'm experiencing a "perfect" moment with my girls and get reminded that their sister is not here. I struggle with the month leading to her birthday as well, but this far into the journey, I at least know to expect that. Time has healed the anger. I think about how much time I spent being angry at family and friends, and realize that, in many cases, I was overly sensitive and expected too much. I did eliminate some friendships, improved others, and created new ones.

Overall, I made it through, and I sincerely want to help others during their difficulties, since I was helped so much during mine. I continue to work on my faith and my confidence that I will see all of my children in heaven one day, and it will be all the sweeter for having them.

Having subsequent children has helped me find purpose again, though I often struggle with questions from my two daughters about their sister. I want them to feel safe and for life to seem fair, at least for a while, but I want them to know that their sister is part of our family. My family NEVER takes our children for granted. They are the stars (and they know it).

My family remembers Amelia by attending a few public ceremonies each year, such as a candlelight ceremony and a Mass. We also spend time at the cemetery and have various graveside activities. We have a personalized wooden memory box. We have many Christmas ornaments for her, and I buy a snow globe for her whenever we are on vacation. My participation on the board of The Still Remembered Project is done in honor of my babies and has increased our attendance at memorial events as well.

My main focus is to make my daughter proud of me. I have a conscious desire to be a better person, though I do not always feel I am achieving this. I know that I am more compassionate, more social, more caring. However, I also feel that I am a more anxious and less confident person than I was before. I think that all of these traits are tied to one single realization: we are not in control. This was something that I had heard before, but never truly owned. I am trying to balance my traits with this in mind and trust in God's plan, even knowing that it is sometimes very difficult.

REMEMBERING BABY AVA
as told by her mother, Kimberly

"As a bereaved mother, I am so often yearning for something to hold onto and something to connect to my baby girl. The photograph that was taken on Mother's Day in memory of my daughter, Ava, is remarkably special and I will treasure it always."

When Kimberly originally received an invitation to partake in a special Mother's Day photo shoot for bereaved mothers, she planned to not participate. After experiencing a miscarriage in January of 2017, when at only seventeen weeks pregnant, the thought of ever having photographs taken never crossed her mind, as she never got to meet or hold her daughter. She felt that by participating, she would be revisiting the pain of losing her daughter, Ava, all over again.

Ironically, the idea of the opportunity never left her thoughts and one particular image cemented in her mind—a simple photograph of her hands holding her daughter's urn that was in the shape of a heart, as a way to remember Ava. Knowing that the photographer was a bereaved mother herself brought a great sense of comfort.

Kimberly's journey with infant loss began on Thursday, January 12, 2017. A routine OB-GYN check-up at seventeen weeks pregnant seemed like the perfect opportunity for Kimberly to take her four-year-old daughter, Annie, along with her to learn about her sibling. She had spent the day sharing the exciting news with her friends and preschool teachers.

In the exam room at the doctor's office, a nurse took Kimberly's vitals while Annie stood at her side, snacking on goldfish crackers, watching every move she made. Kimberly had previously heard her baby's heart beat the month prior and was excited for Annie to hear it, too. The nurse moved the Doppler across the mother's abdomen but could not locate a heartbeat. She tried again, moving carefully and slowly around as little Annie directed her to different spots to try and locate it. The nurse seemed a bit frustrated that she could not pick up a fetal heart beat but Kimberly suggested that perhaps the baby was hiding someplace warm, since it was a dreary, rainy day.

The doctor soon stepped into the room and took over the Doppler. She believed that she had picked up the sound of the baby moving around, but still couldn't find a heartbeat. While she never seemed alarmed, she did move through the rest of the appointment rather quickly and suggested an ultrasound just to be sure that everything was fine. It was late in the day and the only imaging center with an opening was Magee Women's Hospital in Pittsburgh, but Kimberly needed to hurry since the office was thirty minutes away and it was nearing the evening rush hour.

Kimberly remembers feeling inconvenienced on her drive to the hospital, as she had been looking forward to a quiet evening at home with family. "The baby is just fine," she thought to herself over and over again, not the least bit worried. She called her husband, Ethan, who was meeting with a client, to let him know that she and Annie would not be home for dinner.

"When I told Ethan the reason, he told me he would meet me at the hospital. Hearing the bit of panic in his voice almost stunned me and, for the first time, the thought that something might actually be wrong crossed my mind.

"We met at the imaging center and sat in that waiting room for what seemed like forever. Hundreds of different scenarios started playing through my head. Ethan and I had just returned home from Miami, Florida, a couple of days before. While away, I felt the baby really start to move. Now I was sitting as still as I possibly could, waiting to feel any form of movement."

The ultrasound technician finally called Kimberly back and let her know that the appointment was just to confirm a fetal heartbeat and not a full evaluation. She was instructed to lie down on the table and the scan began right away. Ethan, Annie, and Kimberly watched the monitor for what seemed like a split second before the device was quickly removed and the words were said, "I am so sorry, there is no heartbeat."

Kimberly was in utter shock, questioning if she heard correctly?

"The technician let me know that she needed to take some images and asked if I preferred to have the screen shut off. I could not even speak and nodded my head. She asked if I had any questions, and I could barely bring myself to say that I didn't want to ask questions with my daughter in the room, but I wanted to know how many weeks the baby was measuring. She told me that I was measuring around sixteen weeks and she quickly excused herself from the room.

"Ethan was embracing me just as fast as she closed the door behind her. He and I held each other as the tears just poured. All I could think about at that moment was Annie, who was now curled up in a tiny ball on her chair sobbing. I didn't think my heart could break any more at the moment. I had no idea if she was actually comprehending what was going on, or if she was scared seeing Ethan and me so upset. We scooped her into our arms and held her so tight, promising her that mommy was okay."

Soon after, the technician was escorting the family down a hallway, letting Kimberly know that someone would be following up in the morning. She had nothing. Not some kind of care package, not a pamphlet on miscarriages, not a piece of paper, and not even a clue on what to do next.

She remembers that she felt like she was in a shell—empty and hollow.

She picked up her phone and called her mother. All she could muster were the words "there is no heart beat," and she could hear the instant sorrow and equal shock in her mother's gasp.

After the phone call, Annie's big brown eyes looked at her mother and asked, "Is the baby okay?"

"My heart broke even more than it already had in the imaging room. I struggled to find the right words to explain to a four-year-old what was happening. My parents and my sister were at our home when we arrived back later that evening. Perhaps I made conversation, perhaps I just stared blankly at the wall. I can barely even remember the rest of that night, other than calling my very best friend, Alisha, who I met when we attended mortuary school together. She assured me she would handle absolutely everything for me."

The following day was filled with agony as Kimberly waited for a call from the doctor's office. She was scheduled to have a D&E (Dilation and Evacuation), but was informed that she would have to wait an entire week before the surgery the operation. The following days were filled with great despair.

"On one hand, I felt like I needed to hold onto this last week with my baby; on the other, the thought that I was carrying my dead child around inside of me was horrific. I remember stopping at the grocery store during the week and just praying that the cashier did not ask me how I was doing because I wasn't quite sure that I could hold it together. I even went to work for a day because I wanted some sense of normalcy.

"Thursday morning finally arrived. I was sick to my stomach. My heart was racing, my nerves were shot. I was emotionally and mentally exhausted. I had met the doctor performing my surgery the day before at a pre-op consultation appointment, when I had expanders placed inside of my cervix to force dilation. She was very gentle in

21

her delivery of what was going to happen during the surgery. She asked if I would like to have my baby baptized and, if possible, a copy of the baby's hand and foot prints. I could not even formulate the word "yes" through all of the tears. She asked if I had any other questions. I did, just one. The week prior, at my ultrasound appointment, I remembered the technician taking photographs of my baby. I asked if it was at all possible to get a copy of one of those pictures. Several minutes later she came back into my room and handed me an ultrasound picture. The magnitude of that simple act of kindness could never be measured. I had immense gratitude as I was wheeled down to the operating room.

"I left the hospital a couple of hours later with a small white box containing my baby's tiny hand and foot prints. That was all that I had to hold onto of my baby. Not long after I arrived home, my friend, Alisha, called me to let me know she would soon be on her way to pick up my baby to return to the funeral home. I felt so much relief knowing that my baby wasn't going to be left at the hospital overnight and that Alisha was going to take care of my baby.

"Alisha bathed my baby and wrapped her in a small yellow blanket. She prayed over my child and let her know that she is loved deeply. She gifted me with peace of mind like I have never experienced, at the moment when I needed it most. She held my baby on the way to the crematory the following morning, continuing to pray over her. And she kept me updated the entire time until she placed that tiny gold urn into my hands.

"The amount of appreciation and gratitude that I have for Alisha is immeasurable. To this day, when I look at Alisha's hands, I know that those are the only hands to have held my baby. Even I did not have the opportunity to hold my baby in my hands like she did.

"She and I now share matching gold bracelets, each with a single angel wing charm. Wearing mine reminds me not only of my sweet angel baby in heaven, but it also reminds me of the angel that walks along side of me every day, my best friend, Alisha.

"Six weeks later I received a phone call from my surgeon. She let me know that the results of the autopsy were inconclusive and that the actual cause of death was not able to be determined. From all the tests and reports run, everything appeared to be normal. No one had any answers. She asked if I wanted to know the sex of my baby. My heart raced as she told me that I had a baby girl.

"My daughter's name is Ava."

The days, weeks, and months that followed Kimberly's miscarriage were very difficult. There were lots of tears, lots of days of not getting out of bed or off the couch. Her sadness was deeper than she ever experienced before. Not having an answer as to the reason why the pregnancy ended so quickly at seventeen weeks left her feeling incredibly guilty. She had been pregnant before; how could she have not known that something was wrong with her baby?

"Three months after my miscarriage, I drove past a church advertising an upcoming three-part sermon series on grief. Talk about a sign from God. I made a point to be in attendance the following Sunday. As the pastor gave a powerful message, I couldn't take notes fast enough as the tears just ran down my face. The following two Sunday's he delivered more sermons that left me equally as moved. Each week he would mention the book, *Through the Eyes of a Lion* by Levi Lusko. On the third Sunday, I had ordered the book before leaving the church parking lot.

"As soon as the book arrived, I settled in to begin reading it. The words in that book completely transformed my grief journey. I left several pages marked with bright pink highlighter. The author's words spoke directly to my heart: my pain was a microphone and my suffering was an opportunity to share my story and God's love with others. I found hope in knowing that in the future, I would be able to see the transformation from a mess to a masterpiece, and that my story could help to shine light into the darkness of others. I refused to not let something absolutely wonderful happen out of my heartbreak. I felt empowered in my grief."

More than two years have passed since Ava was born and those devastating words "there is no heartbeat" still echo in the back of Kimberly's mind. The sadness is still there and the month of January seems to hit the hardest.

Kimberly found a wonderful support in The Still Remembered Project, where she could pour out her heart in a safe and non-judgmental environment, and not feel ashamed for still grieving.

"Receiving support from the efforts of The Still Remembered Project has been incredibly healing in my grief journey. Most important to me, is that by being a part of this community of hope, my daughter lives.

"As the adage goes, 'the more you give, the more you will receive,' I have found this to be especially true in my grief journey. I have worked to help raise awareness of The Still Remembered Project and offer my own resources to support the organization any way that I can. I always send a highlighted copy of *Through the Eyes of a Lion* to mothers who I learn have just experienced a miscarriage. Despite the sadness, I am filled with hope and gratitude—and I know that by being there for others, I am actually healing myself."

JOURNAL PROMPT

Do you remember struggling to find support, or the sense of "coming up empty," or feeling alone after your loss?

CHAPTER 2

SILENT GRIEF

"Just when I think that I've cried all the tears that I have inside, there are always more that come without warning. And another day goes by that I haven't made it through without crying."

Months after losing my infant twins, a journal entry showed that the words would not come. There was nothing to say—a lack of language to process what had happened.

In the early days and weeks that follow the loss of an infant, bereaved mothers often express how they went through the motions of life and suffered in silence.

REMEMBERING CHRISTOPHER,
as told by his mother, Lynn

"As a practicing social worker, I learned to sit with the incredible grief of my clients, to support them, not judge, to give the space and time to express the depth of feeling and honor their loss, no matter what age or circumstance."

Lynn gave birth to twin boys, Christopher and Matthew, at thirty-two weeks' gestational age in 1989. At the time, she worked as a psychiatric social worker in a community hospital in Pittsburgh. The entire hospital staff knew of her twin pregnancy and would ask daily about her health and the boys.

"We made the heartbreaking decision to disconnect Christopher's life support at seventeen days after the boys' birth. News of the tragedy spread fast.

"When I returned to work four months later, the hospital staff either avoided me or only wanted to talk about my son, Matthew. I brought a book of pictures from the first four months that included pictures of both boys in the NICU, and my social work supervisor boldly told me that the staff didn't like seeing pictures of Christopher. I told him that was their problem and that I was a mother of two boys, one living and one deceased."

Lynn remembers that sometimes she would use stark language to shock people on purpose and shatter the silence that surrounded infant death. Insensitive comments like, "at least you have a living son," were heard often. People seemed to ignore the fact that she was devastated by the loss of the baby she buried. No one wants to acknowledge infant death—it is too threatening.

The most sensitive comment she can remember receiving was from one of the nurses on her unit. She said, "I don't even know what to say to you. When I think about you, I think about my own two boys and what it would be like to lose one. Then I start crying. I can't even imagine what this must feel like for you."

Her coworker's willingness to speak those words to Lynn was the acknowledgement she wanted and needed. She did hurt, every single day. She went to work every day and did her job, often crying in her car during the thirty-minute drive from home to work.

A supervisor told her that a colleague's infertility and early miscarriages were worse than her loss. That colleague had suffered visibly at work while Lynn covered up her own suffering. Lynn told her supervisor that as a social worker, she was surprised that he would judge one's loss as better or worse than another. She told him that she cried every day in her car, and when she felt like she could not go on another day, she would go into her surviving son's room and watch him sleep.

"I told myself that Matthew deserved a mother that was present for him, that I had to live and function for him," Lynn recalls. "I finally joined Compassionate Friends, and that helped. As a practicing social worker, I learned to sit with the incredible grief of my clients, to support them, not judge, to give the space and time to express the depth of feeling and honor their loss, no matter what age or circumstance." She knew she also had to do that for herself, even if others could not.

In some ways, Lynn feels fortunate. When she celebrates Matthew's birthday, it is also Christopher's. Matthew is now thirty and has mild cerebral palsy as a result of his premature birth. He was raised with the knowledge that his twin brother died as a baby. Lynn's parents had lost a baby boy as well, so the families have always honored the two boys. They understand, but many do not, even many professionals.

REMEMBERING AN INFANT DAUGHTER LOST AT TWENTY WEEKS,
as told by her mother, Gail

"There is no one to tell this to unless they have been through it. Thank you for allowing us to grieve our newborns no longer with us."

After years of trying to conceive, Gail was pregnant in 1983, having been married for ten years. In the early hours of Monday, February 27, at three a.m., Gail's water broke. She questioned, how could this be? She was only twenty weeks along in the pregnancy.

She called the doctor and was told to get to the hospital immediately. They put a fetal monitor on her, and Gail could hear the heartbeat. She had been seeing a group of doctors in a practice and had met each of them by this time. One of the physicians came in after about five hours, put his hand on Gail's, and said, "I think you're going to lose this baby."

"I can't," Gail said. "I have waited too long."

Along with her amniotic fluid leaking out, tears were streaming down her face. They waited for her to start dilating, but she didn't. One senior nurse came in with a student, and the experienced nurse asked the doctor to remove the fetal monitor.

"It was just too heartbreaking," she remembers. "The doctor asked the student nurse to leave because she started crying."

30

So, the wait started. The other doctors from the group came in. One of them kindly assured Gail that she would be OK and have another baby. He explained that they would try to save this baby, but the chances were small and that there would be great medical concerns. Gail and her husband agreed that they did not want to use extraordinary measures to save the baby.

Another physician came in and was most compassionate. Gail asked if this procedure would be considered an abortion. She was Catholic. The physician said that it was called a "premature delivery." And so they waited.

Finally, near five p.m., Gail began to dilate. Her husband called a cousin, who was a nun, to be with them and baptize the baby. She was also the only family member nearby. She came immediately.

As with all labor, the contractions were painful. They had everyone leave the room and administered an epidural. At 9:02 p.m. a daughter was born, eighteen ounces and oh, so tiny.

"They asked me if I wanted to hold her, but I said 'no' because I would never let her go," Gail said. "Our baby was baptized, and that was it. They were going to put me on the maternity floor, but that would have been too cruel. I do not know who spoke up. They put me in a regular room for the night instead. The next morning, my husband brought me clothes, and my jeans did not fit. Then a social worker came in, but I dismissed her. I just wanted to go home. We were told that we had to make funeral arrangements. We went to a store to buy a white infant blanket to wrap her in and went to the funeral home. She was buried in the Cemetery of Angels in her own little coffin."

Gail stayed home from work for a week until her breasts stopped leaking.

"I just felt so empty."

She describes herself as a mental mess for two years. She struggled to get pregnant again and finally asked her gynecologist if he thought she needed mental help. His words were the wisest words she has ever heard:

"You need mental help when you have nothing to look forward to," the physician said. Those words changed Gail's life.

Gail and her husband decided to adopt instead, and their son arrived in 1987 as a five-month-old beautiful little boy. They never again conceived a biological child.

"After more than three decades, gallons of tears, and always in our prayers, our daughter is never forgotten. Thank you. Speaking of this has been cathartic."

REMEMBERING BABY CAROLINE,
as told by her mother, Kelly

"She was very sick, but I would have taken her home any way she was, any way at all. With grief—you are so busy doing what you're supposed to be doing with life, that it's only in these quiet moments that it sneaks up on you, when you least expect it. Or, when it's not so quiet, it will hit or you will think about it."

 For the longest time, I couldn't listen to my own story that was recorded for a podcast about the loss of my infant daughter, Caroline.

I've always loved the name "Caroline" so I had given her that name and was looking forward to meeting the person who would have that.

We had pulled up to the emergency room, and the nurses asked, "What baby is this?" and when I answered that this was my first child, I felt like they dismissed me for overreacting to labor. But when the nurses picked up the bed sheet and realized that the baby was crowning, they immediately rushed me to the delivery room. I think I was in shock and didn't realize what was going on.

I had precipitous labor so everything happened so quickly. I had no signs of labor and then, within an hour, so much had happened: I was spotting, my water broke, the baby was crowning, her head was out, and when she was born, her color was terrible. It was a whirlwind. All of a sudden, a lot of doctors and nurses were in the room, and when she was born, they took Caroline straight to intensive care. Then they started explaining to me that she was not alright. No one knew exactly what happened during her birth, but she clearly lost a lot of oxygen to her brain.

I remember thinking, "She's lost oxygen. She's really sick," but I thought she'd be paralyzed. I was signing papers with the social worker and thinking it was bad, but that she'd be really sick. I never thought that she wasn't going to survive.

I told my doctor, "I didn't even get to see her," and then she did a wonderful thing. She took Caroline's picture on a Polaroid camera and brought it to me. I later remember walking into the neonatal intensive care unit, and the head of that unit asked me if we were ready to take Caroline off life support.

I was completely shocked and broke down in tears. At that point, I didn't know we would be facing that decision. She was very sick, but I would have taken her home any way she was, any way at all.

They sent me into another room saying that I was disturbing other parents. A really nice nurse came in and talked to us. She realized we needed time before we could make a decision to take her off life support. I was frantically searching for any signs that she would start to wake up. Her heart and lungs were getting stronger.

A couple of days went by as they did numerous tests. They showed that she had severe brain damage. The doctors definitively said they did not think she would recover any brain function. This was not like a parent or a spouse where you would have had a conversation and known their wishes in a situation like this, or at least you knew them as a person, and you could speculate on what they would want. You have some way to make a more informed decision. I had none of that. My daughter couldn't tell me what she wanted, and that really, really weighed on me.

So we talked to a priest, and from the Catholic perspective, he said it was not like we were taking life in a bad way. So my husband and I made the decision to take her off life support. We set a time and invited some friends and family to come and say hello and goodbye to Caroline. They finally unhooked all the machines, and it was actually the only time I was able to hold her. And that was wonderful for me to be able to do that.

I was thirty-six-years old when I became a mother in 1999. Within seventy-two hours of Caroline's birth, I was still in shock. Looking back, I wished there had been more time for decisions and that I would not been rushed to judgement—more space so I could feel more certain that it was the right thing to do.

And no one tells you what that's like. You have no idea. You just can't imagine. There was such a whirlwind of emotion. Without the tubes, Caroline didn't look sick. She was perfect and beautiful. I just wanted to take her home, but then I just wanted the situation to be over. It was just the two of us. She passed away, and we asked for an autopsy to see what contributed to this. We wanted to know if this was something genetic. We learned later there was no apparent cause of death. I still believe it was because the labor was much too fast. I kept thinking maybe if I had gone to a closer hospital we could have delivered her sooner. The guessing is torture.

I remember my own mother had lost an infant son (my baby brother) the day he was born. Childbirth was not very easy for her and as a result, she was worried about me. I remember thinking, "I cannot bury my child. I just can't." We had a service for her, but when it came time to go to the cemetery, I didn't think I could go to the grave, but my maternal instinct was too strong, and I did get out of the car. I was in rough shape for a long time. I did seek help and therapy. I was hungry to find anyone who understood, and back then, there was no group for people like me. I wondered, "Where is a group for people who lost babies?"

People made insensitive comments. One said, "That's nothing. Be glad she didn't live any longer." I resented the idea that people could compare because everyone's situation is different whether it's a miscarriage, an adult child, a baby born too early. You can't compare as if it's a small, medium, or large grief. I just felt so isolated.

Then I was pregnant with my son and had to focus on that. It was incredibly scary. I was a high risk pregnancy and they had planned to induce me early so I wouldn't go into labor on my own.

When I was in labor with my son, I remember thinking, "I am having a baby, but will I take this baby home?"

That's how it is with grief. You are so busy doing what you're supposed to be doing with life, that it's only in these quiet moments that it sneaks up on you, or something you don't expect will trigger the grief.

I told Ethan about his sister Caroline when he was four or five years old, and he didn't really get it. My stepdaughter was always upset that she never had the chance to see Caroline, or to say goodbye, or have closure. She had always wanted a sister. If I had to do it over, I probably would have done it differently.

I find it so sad that mothers go through that. They question what they did and wonder what they could have done.

If you find someone who has been in your shoes, you don't feel so isolated.

One of the most healing things for me was telling the story whenever I found someone to listen. For me, that was also keeping her memory alive, and that really helped me a lot. I would talk about Caroline whenever and wherever I could.

Just know that if you get to a point where you can share your story, you are certainly helping someone else because no one is ever ready to go through this. The sense of isolation you feel is overwhelming. So if you can share, someone else won't feel alone. You'll be a comfort to them, and no doubt, you'll feel less alone yourself. It's somehow reassuring to know that someone else has walked in your shoes.

JOURNAL PROMPT

How did you react during the first few days after the loss of your infant? What can you share about your jourey of grief?

CHAPTER 3

CARRIED WITHIN YOU
THE FABRIC OF WHO YOU ARE

The question is repeated in the mind of a bereaved parent: "If I let go and quit remembering, will my child cease to exist?"

The truth is, the deep sense of absence will always be there—becoming a placeholder for the child that you carried within you and lost.

Joann Cantrell

REMEMBERING PETER STEPHEN,
as told by his mother Anne Jane

"It's not daily dwelling. It's the fabric of who you are. It is something you carry always. It was good to actually think about my baby, Peter, right now—to embrace him and think about the child he might have been. So it was not bad going back there. People go through so many hardships in life. I felt like it made me more part of the human race to suffer such deep grief and understand more about what other people felt. One would never choose it, but it made me a better human being and more empathetic."

Anne Jane's first son, Peter Stephen, died at six days old in the 1980s. He was born early, and while he was a fairly good size for his age, he suffered Respiratory Distress Syndrome (RDS), a breathing disorder that affects newborns and eventually caused a brain bleed. He was born just a little too soon for the medical advances that that may have been able to keep him alive.

"At that time, we lived in Urbana, Illinois, and the hospital there was very supportive. They let us hold him as he died. The hospital later put us in touch with a group of grieving parents. We also were part of a babysitting co-op and another family in that group had suffered a stillbirth near the same time. We learned very quickly that pregnancy does not always go the way we wish."

Peter was the firstborn for Anne Jane and her husband Dave. It was a perfectly normal pregnancy with no indication that anything was wrong, although Anne Jane went into labor early, at seven months. At first, the doctors thought she had a urinary tract infection, but when she ended up in the hospital, they discovered she was in labor and performed a C-section.

Peter was four pounds, two ounces, and he was in the NICU for the few days he was alive. He was doing well, but the doctors warned that he had lung disease and was very sick. Along with the RDS syndrome, he had a brain bleed and a stroke.

"The doctors called us in to say that Peter was not going to survive. I remember it was a beautiful sunny day in October. I had gone home after I had him and traveled back and forth to stay with him. They were going to take him off the respirator, and they let us hold him. He died in our arms. Peter had tubes all over him and the staff took great care to clean him and take a photograph for us. They were very supportive. But you have second thoughts and many 'whys?'. I still feel shell-shocked by it."

Anne Jane and her husband had a strong compulsion to return home to Pittsburgh to be near family. Anne Jane's in-laws had a plot in a cemetery, and arrangements were made to bury Peter there. The bereaved parents made the long drive from Illinois with their baby in a tiny coffin, staying overnight in a motel. To have their son there with them was so precious, as they had their own private good-bye.

"We had a little ceremony and stayed in Pittsburgh for several days. I remember taking a little outfit to the funeral home and a toy to put in the coffin. When we came back to Illinois, they connected us with a program called SHARE. At the time, it was one of the only groups for those who had lost a child.

"I remember going into the room that would have been the baby's room. Someone had given us handmade stuffed toys, and when I saw them, I just cried and cried for the child that would never be there.

"Initially, we hid. We watched movies. We didn't go out. We were like animals licking our wounds. We just let it wash over us. We let ourselves grieve, and I think that was a good thing. I kept wishing the seasons would go by quickly, but time felt endless.

"I remember receiving a card from someone that said, 'It's better that he died because he had the brain bleed, and he would have been mentally incapacitated.' They may have meant well, but that was tough.

"And we were on tenterhooks around our friends who had kids, but that was me more than them. People didn't know what to say.

"We were fortunate to have two more sons in 1986 and 1989. They are grown men now, but we have always kept the photo of Peter Stephen on our dresser, so he remains part of our family.

"Some years, Mother's Day bothers me, or on All Souls Day, I do think about him. But it was good to actually think about him right now—to really think about him. I haven't done that in years. And to embrace him and think about the child he might have been. So it was not bad going back there. People go through so many hardships in life. I felt like it made me more part of the human race to suffer such deep grief and understand more about what other people felt. One would never choose it, but it made me a better human being and more empathetic.

"I can talk about it now, but still, deep down inside you feel the loss of that child that you never knew. When we first lost Peter, I remember seeing kids in the grocery store and feeling sad, wondering why we couldn't have kids. Every year on the anniversary of his death, both of us still feel blue.

"It's not daily dwelling. It's the fabric of who you are. It is something you carry.

"After our loss, I knew we had choices. One was to wallow there and get pulled down, or to make something of it—to find some usefulness or purpose. I don't believe everything happens for a reason, but maybe I could come out stronger. Like if you injure yourself, for a while you are weaker but sometimes in the end you can exercise and come out stronger. I knew if we could get through this and let ourselves grieve, we could move from it with a new purpose and strength.

"I would be happy if I could help a newly bereaved mother. Life isn't fair, but I think it was a valuable lesson to learn. I made the choice to make peace with it and not be bitter. For some, it would be really hard to come out on the other side. I was lucky I had a lot of support, especially from my husband.

"If I were to tell mothers in the same situation anything, I would say to take the time they need to let the wounds heal. Embrace the grief and think about their child and know that they'll carry that child with them for the rest of their life. It's both sad and beautiful in a way."

REMEMBERING BABY KARL,
a letter on miscarriage from his mother Tracy

"Support and lean on each other, and understand that men and women grieve differently. Losing a child is the most difficult of all the types of grief I've experienced. It is a loss of your future, your hopes and dreams for your life with this child. Don't let anyone get to you with their delusional ideas that it didn't matter because you never knew the child, as many people have said to me. They have NO IDEA what they are talking about!"

I know how devastating the grief from losing a baby is. The depth of grief and longing for the empty space left behind is gut-wrenching.

I wanted to share a little about my experience. In July of 1992, I found out through an ultrasound that the child I carried was dead at sixteen weeks. After that appointment, I had to drive across Phoenix to pick up my husband from work. It is a wonder that I made it without wrecking.

I had to wait a week for the appointment to induce labor because the Air Force OB doctor was on temporary duty elsewhere, and we had a visiting OB who only came once a week. I don't remember that week much. They induced labor using a Pitocin IV drip and were considerate enough to put me in a ward that had been closed off, so I would not be around the other mothers on the OB ward.

The labor was long and difficult, despite the baby not being full term. They ended up having to do a D&C because of bleeding that wouldn't stop, and I also had a transfusion. We were fortunate to be able to hold Baby Karl, who was smaller than my hand. It would have been tremendously worse to be around all of the happy new parents.

Afterwards, I was off work for two weeks. I think I cried the entire time. One of my strongest memories from that time was that I had to call everyone to tell them we lost the baby. The first thing my mother-in-law said to me was, "What did you do?" At the time, I did not appreciate that she was also grieving, but I have never forgotten that moment when she clearly blamed me for the loss. My husband and I had been living ultra-healthy, from a diet high in fresh vegetables to many workouts and hikes in the desert, and nothing we did caused the miscarriage. There was a group at the hospital called "Resolve with Sharing" that made home visits and did grief counseling. That was very helpful.

For the next several months, I could hardly stand to look at strollers or baby items, much less be around people who had small children. (A difficult proposition since we lived on an Air Force base with tons of families with little ones.) It takes a bit of time to get over that feeling.

Meditation and reflection helped, as well as talking with friends and the Resolve visitor. She made sure we had mementos of our son. The grief from this pregnancy loss, in particular, revisits from time to time, just as any grief does.

I know that my grandmother still grieved for her lost babies, even sixty years later. Even in her eighties, when we had long talks about genealogy and family information, she would become teary-eyed over John, her one-year-old who had died from pneumonia, and Louise, who had been stillborn. Many would have assumed that their loss didn't matter because she had ten living children at the time.

Our society blames women for many things, and this is one situation that I ran into from more people than just my mother-in-law. One of the surgeons at the Air Force base hospital that I knew glared at me for the rest of my time at Luke Air Force Base. I felt tremendous relief years later when I discovered that I had Factor V Leiden, a genetic blood clotting disorder that was responsible for the recurrent pregnancy losses, of which I had seven, including Karl, who was the first.

Even asking me how many children I have is a loaded question. I always want to ask people if they want to know how many living children I have or how many total. Many people feel compelled to comment on the fact that my two living children are nine years apart. It is very awkward to inform them that I lost many babies in the years between them, and I generally don't tell them.

Now, I usually have to discuss the pregnancy loss at medical appointments, especially with a new provider. It never fails to bother me that medical records call it an "abortion," since I did not have an abortion, only a D&C after delivery, and had several miscarriages, typically at ten to twelve weeks each.

Please allow yourself time to grieve. You may not experience everything I've described, but everyone, and every couple is different. It is NOT your fault. Support and lean on each other, and understand that men and women grieve differently.

Losing a child is the most difficult of all the types of grief I've experienced. It is a loss of your future, your hopes and dreams for your life with this child. Don't let anyone get to you with their delusional ideas that it didn't matter because you never knew the child, as many people have said to me. They have NO IDEA what they are talking about!

Have a ceremony or funeral, and make a memory book. Meditate. Don't judge yourselves; just let yourselves experience this journey together until you come out on the other side. It will take time. You will never be back to normal, but you will find a new normal.

JOURNAL PROMPT

What is the story that will be carried within you? What do you want others to know about your pregnancy and infant loss?

CHAPTER 4

THE NEED FOR UNDERSTANDING
"SAY ANYTHING."

For many bereaved parents, when the fog finally lifts, there is a yearning for the need to have their baby acknowledged and to share and talk of the experience and unthinkable journey.

The reminders are constant. Particularly in the seasons or anything that validates that life goes on. This is especially true in hearing the news that another woman is pregnant or seeing babies in strollers or tiny clothes on display in a store.

While it may seem as if a bereaved mother is going through life with the sound muted, there is a strong need for understanding and wanting others to say something.

REMEMBERING CAMERON JOSEPH,
as told by his mother, Kelly

"I'm grateful I had the opportunity to spend the greatest day of my life with him. Growing him in my belly and then meeting him made me realize there is this unbelievable love you never knew you were capable of."

My son's name is Cameron Joseph. He was diagnosed at our eighteen-week ultrasound after the doctor noticed his kidneys were slightly enlarged, and we were referred to a specialist on February 20, 2016. That was the day my grieving began. It was the second worst day of my life.

We were told that Cameron had a rare genetic kidney disease called Autosomal Recessive Polycystic Kidney Disease (ARPKD), which affects one in twenty thousand. The doctor actually told us we had a better chance of winning the lottery. My husband, Todd, and I had no known family history of kidney issues, so we were baffled. It was as if our baby was given a death sentence, but we could only get updates at our ultrasound appointment every three weeks. We were given very little information as they didn't know enough about the disease.

It was up to us to do all of the research. This disease causes the loss of amniotic fluid and as a result, the baby's lungs do not develop. Lung immaturity is the main cause of death in infants with ARPKD.

Throughout the remainder of the pregnancy, we met with NICU docs, specialists at Children's Hospital and genetic doctors. Despite Cameron requiring dialysis and one or more transplants down the road, we were given a positive outlook by a few physicians. A few doctors even told us we were on the less severe side of this disease, and I had sufficient fluid past the critical point of lung development. I did not run out until thirty-one weeks.

At our 37.5-week ultrasound appointment, they decided to induce me. We had a normal delivery, and he scored a seven on the APGAR test (an assessment of overall newborn well-being) but was immediately whisked away to the NICU. We were able to see Cameron later that evening and were told he was responding well to treatment. But we were not out of the woods yet, due to his lungs being underdeveloped. The next morning, a NICU doctor came up to my room, and I had this horrible feeling when I saw her face. She told us that, overnight, things took a turn for the worse, and he was dying.

We were told to invite family to come in and say their goodbyes. We had to sign off on papers to take him off life support. He passed in our arms that afternoon. I remember holding him while seeing him change colors due to the lack of oxygen in his brain, and he grew cold. He was born June 9, 2016, and passed June 10, 2016.

Coming home from the hospital that day, entering his nursery nearly killed me. I seriously thought I would pass out from the sadness. It felt as if someone had kicked me in the stomach and my heart was ripped out. I couldn't breathe and was sobbing hysterically.

I was on a rollercoaster of emotions, and I still fluctuate between stages of grief. I realize that not every person grieves the same way, and I felt very guilty for quite a long time. As Cameron's mother, I felt that I was a failure and should have been able to protect him.

In addition to losing a child, your body is also going through so many changes with hormones. Your body and emotions already have a mind of their own at this time, so throwing in bereavement takes it to another level. I was angry a lot and kept (and still keep) a mental scorecard of who reached out and who didn't. I remember the first few days after returning from the hospital just lying in bed with the TV on. I cannot remember what was on. I just stared at the wall in a catatonic state. I think part of me was in shock. I was also worried I would forget about what our little guy looked like because of the limited time spent with him.

I never even heard from some of our friends and family. I battled bouts of depression and anxiety. I purposely avoided going out in public to avoid the potential of running into people I knew. I would hide in the car and refuse to get out and go in the grocery store or Target. I didn't want to have to explain myself. From the Subway sandwich girl to the trolley driver, I was asked about Cameron. I couldn't escape it.

For a short period, I thought about ending everything but never acted upon it. I cried over everything and felt worthless. I believed that everything was my fault. I hated myself. I'm unsure if it was postpartum depression or just depression in general. The next month, I knew I needed help.

Upon seeking outpatient therapy, I was medicated with Paxil, and that took the edge off. It was good and bad. I was feeling better but also needed to feel those raw emotions to process my grief. I returned to work less than two months after Cameron's passing.

Most of our patients knew what happened while I was gone, but many didn't. I had patients give me their condolences, and others would make it seem like it was just a fluke. Many, would say, "You're young still," or wave their hand and say, "Oh, you can always have another," making it seem like my son's life was a bus pass and I can always get a new one. Or, "I didn't know you named it." I had patients bring in gifts for Cameron. All the while, I would slap on this smile and say, "Thank you so much." Every day for months, I would go home and cry for hours. Just because he was a baby doesn't mean I didn't have a chance to bond with him.

I think back to when my grandparents were children. Infant death was very common. But they were "programmed" not to discuss it. My grandma had two sisters who died shortly after birth and under the age of two. I remember as a kid, her telling me about them. I'm glad she did. When she referred to having sisters, she talked about having four instead of just the two who were living.

While on leave from work after losing my son, I didn't even hear from my coworkers. Not a card, phone call, or text. I was beyond hurt. These were people I have supported over the years and have been there for them through surgeries, losses, and breakups. Biting my tongue through an entire workday, in addition to being disgusted by the lack of actions from my coworkers was killing me. I was having chest pains and panic attacks. I remember hiding in our supply closet because I was SO angry.

I would smell Cameron's onesie he wore in the hospital almost every day and remember falling apart the day it didn't carry his scent anymore. When patients or strangers weren't fair or very nice to me, I would think, "Don't you know what I've been through? Cut me some slack, and just be kind. I'm very fragile."

I checked myself into outpatient hospital therapy for four to five weeks, with weekly counseling. My husband and family were nothing short of amazing. Every day before outpatient therapy, my mom and cousin would call or text and tell me how proud they were of me for seeking help. My family tried to keep me busy and was there for me the whole time. I didn't have to explain or justify any of my emotions; they allowed me to know that my feelings were valid and reiterated that I will always be Cameron's mom. They got me out of the house and took me walking, to the zoo, lunch, park, etc. A few of my friends were so amazing. Most of them had moved away and asked if I wanted them to fly in. They were so supportive, checking in on me each day.

A friend suggested I attend a meeting of The Still Remembered Project (SRP) shortly after Cameron passed. Attending this meeting with other bereaved moms gave me another sense of camaraderie—one that was more relatable. Meeting with other moms and knowing how they felt and what they experienced, was comforting in a sad way. I hate that I met these women under these circumstances, but these are some of the strongest women you will ever meet in your life. They are supportive, and your feelings are validated, no matter what they may be.

My family played the biggest role in my healing. They allowed me to be me and to feel what I was feeling. They were a constant support system, and I needed that. I went through some extremely dark periods in the beginning. I felt empty and crestfallen. I did feel alone, but it was not because family wasn't there, but because I felt as if no one (outside SRP) could possibly understand what I was going through. My future was taken away from me, just like that. Seeing babies and little kids with their parents gave me the "what could have been" thoughts. Most people have not had their child suffer and die in their arms. It's a moment I think about all the time.

I wish more people had said something. Anything. I never did hear from some friends and family who I thought would have been front and center. Then, some people I haven't spoken to in years reached out via social media just to say they were thinking of me, and that meant a lot.

There's something very taboo about infant loss. It's as if people almost think the quality of life isn't there because they are so young, and that's not okay. He was our child, no matter how long he lived in my belly and on this earth. People didn't know what to say. I think it's always better to say anything than nothing. Just let someone know you are thinking about them.

It was also extremely important to hear people say his name, instead of "the baby." Cameron was our first and only pregnancy or child. During the pregnancy, Todd and I were at odds ninety percent of the time. It was like we were living in a pressure cooker since February 20th. We were told our son would probably die, and there was nothing we could do about it. We were under an unbelievable amount of stress. When he was positive, I was negative, and vice versa. He didn't want to hear about how I handled work when patients or anyone else would ask about my pregnancy. He said the negativity was too much for him. He joined an online support group of parents whose children passed away or are currently living with ARPKD. He would talk about it nonstop, and I almost felt as if he would be open with his feelings to these strangers, but not with me.

I felt as if he was creating a sense of false hope, while I thought I was being realistic, knowing the inevitable. Toward the end of our pregnancy, things changed completely. We came to this sudden understanding. We were all our little guy had, and we needed to get it together.

Your future is ripped away from you. You see this tiny, innocent human who depended on you their entire life gasping for air, being taken away. It is the cruelest thing you can imagine. Holding your child and watching them die, knowing you can't do a damn thing. We had Cameron baptized before he passed. The NICU nurse came in and suggested we take professional pictures, and a gentleman there took some for our memories. At first, I thought this was nuts. I was still in complete shock. My husband wasn't really onboard. I thought it was sort of morbid. We were wrong. We will forever cherish our pictures with him. I was able to change him, which I was so grateful for. The hospital gave us a memory box with his footprint, a bracelet with his name on it, and baptism gown and encouraged us to create memories, otherwise we wouldn't have had the chance to.

We had a funeral for Cameron, and he is buried with my grandmother and next to my grandfather. Selecting his burial outfit and which stuffed toys to bury with him was agonizing. On Christmas Eve, we let balloons go in his honor at the cemetery.

With the anniversary of his birthday and death approaching, I don't know what to expect or how I will feel. I may lie in bed all day. I may get a cake and have our family over. This has changed me for the better and worse. I feel like a part of me is gone, possibly one of the best parts of me has died with him. My anxiety is worse. I value the relationships I do have dearly. I've let go of some relationships that were probably just not meant to be.

I'm grateful I had the opportunity to spend the greatest day of my life with him. Growing him in my belly and then meeting him made me realize there is this unbelievable love you never knew you were capable of. Our marriage is stronger than ever. I hold my husband in the highest regard. Sometimes I look at him and just think, "Wow, you gave me the greatest gift in the entire world. You allowed me to be a mom to Cameron." Today, our marriage has never been stronger.

REMEMBERING ETHAN PATRICK AND CASEY LAWRENCE,
as told by their mother, Erin

"I don't know when a shift happened, outside of realizing I needed to talk to someone. I looked for a psychologist who specialized in women's issues, something a friend of mine had recommended, and made an appointment. I don't remember how I felt after that first appointment, but I do know that I was comforted in knowing I finally had someone to talk to."

My babies' names are Ethan Patrick and Casey Lawrence—twin boys who were born very prematurely on March 7, 2007, at just twenty-weeks and five days, far too early to survive.

Looking back, I should have recognized something wasn't right. I don't know why the on-and-off lower back pains I had the afternoon of March 6 did not concern me. I don't know why I didn't mention it to my boss at the time, who most certainly would have ushered me to the hospital across the river to be checked. I don't know why my mom reflexes didn't kick in. Perhaps if they had, doctors could have prolonged my pregnancy, and my sons would be here. Would have, could have, should have. These are statements to which I'll never have the answers.

After my water broke at home the evening of March 6, I called an ambulance, which rushed me to Allegheny General Hospital. I remember the EMT (emergency medical technician) congratulating me, and me telling him "No, it was much too early." My OB-GYN was on call that night. I remember the flurry of activity—being whisked to my room and having people come out of nowhere. In came

57

my OB to check me. I asked if my babies were going to be OK. One young resident put her head down and shook her head no. My world was crashing—and I was in shock.

My husband, who was nine hundred miles away in Florida for work, called our brother-in-law to stay with me at the hospital until my mom and brother arrived. This would be the second hospital in two weeks that my mom and brother had rushed to as my dad had died suddenly twelve days earlier.

I delivered my sons naturally in the early morning hours of March 7th. Ethan, my first, was born sleeping. Casey stuck around in my womb kicking for a while, and then his water broke. He was delivered alive. I will never forget him taking a big gulp of air while his little hands rose high. I can still hear it. The doctor handed him to me, and I just stared at him. I'm not sure why I didn't take him and interact with him while he was still alive. It's something I'll regret for the rest of my life. He passed away while under the warmer.

My babies. Gone. Just like that—the babies who took several years to become a reality through fertility treatments. The little boys we had such high hopes for were now gone. Now angels. And no one knew why it happened.

I'm still on my grief journey more than ten years later. It's a train I would like to have never boarded, but I guess we don't always get to choose our paths in life.

In the early days of my grief journey, I was in a complete fog. I didn't know which end was up; didn't care about anything. I was constantly questioning why—why me? Why my sons? Hadn't my family just been through enough losing my dad so suddenly? We wanted those babies so badly; we had such plans for the family of four that we were supposed to be.

Once the fog wore off, anger set in. I was angry at myself and my body. I was angry at my husband for not talking and for bottling things up and locking it away. I was angry at God. I hated life. I hit things. I threw things. I screamed. I hollered. I tried to make sense of what happened. But what sense is there when your children are taken away?

I took three weeks off after we lost the boys. My husband's employer paid for me to return to Florida with him. The time away did me good, but I spent a lot of time alone. I didn't interact with others much. Nothing mattered but the hell I was living.

I don't know when a shift happened, outside of realizing I needed to talk to someone. I asked my OB-GYN for the number of a psychologist who specialized in women's issues, something a friend of mine had recommended. It turned out that another of my OB-GYN's patients was a psychologist. I called her immediately and made an appointment. I don't remember how I felt after that first appointment, but I do know that I felt comforted in knowing I finally had someone to talk to. She, and a subsequent therapist, as well as the March of Dimes Share Your Story, pulled me through an experience I wish no one ever had to live through.

There are times and days that hit hard. The wave can hit unexpectedly, but it can also be triggered by a certain song, or as the calendar turns to the new year. It's a journey that has taught me a lot about myself and about what really matters in life, but I sometimes wish I didn't have these insights. I wish I could still be naïve and think that every pregnancy has a happy ending.

It's been more than ten years since my loss. With each passing year, the pain of the loss still hits hard, although with less severity than the first year. But even though the ache isn't as sharp, each year puts me farther and farther away from remembering what it felt like to feel them moving inside of me...to feel them in my arms...to touch their faces...to kiss them. I thought that ten years would be hard to swallow this year, and it was, but less emotional, which surprised me. It was also ten years since my father died, and I found myself more emotional because I never had time to grieve my dad with losing my twins so close.

I was frustrated after my loss that the hospital I delivered at didn't provide a list of support groups for perinatal or baby loss. I researched the information myself and shared it with the hospital, my OB-GYN, and the local March of Dimes chapter. I wasn't the first mother who experienced such a loss and I surely wouldn't be the last, so I hoped that it would help someone who came after me.

The March of Dimes Share your Story website, share.marchofdimes.org, was and is my lifesaver, as the online community was full of moms and dads just like me, trying to navigate their new normal. Share was a place I could go and write out my deepest fears, triumphs, tears and everything in between. I wasn't judged. It was my safe place (and still is). It was a place I could feel close to my sons and their story.

I did attend a few face-to-face support group sessions, but I was further along in my grief journey than the others, and I realized that I needed to stay with the one-on-one therapy sessions. I had to switch psychologists, as the original one became pregnant, and it was too much seeing her in that state. She referred me to another one, who I saw up until April 2010—a month after my rainbow daughter,

---

[1] A baby born subsequent to a miscarriage, stillbirth, or the death of an infant from natural causes.

Kaelin, was born. This second doctor kept me sane throughout my pregnancy.

The second psychologist I saw also made a huge impact. Unlike the first doctor who felt more like a friend (which I needed at the time), this one truly made me work and drove my healing process. She kept me sane in my ongoing fertility struggles, which included having to go through IVF (in vitro fertilization) to have my rainbow daughter. She taught me coping strategies, and encouraged me to set a goal to relax, breathe, and enjoy that pregnancy.

At home, though, I felt like I was on an island. My husband was seemingly going about his life like nothing had happened. He went back to work two days after he returned home. He kept saying "I don't need to talk to anyone." Well, not talking also extended to me, unfortunately.

There were many things that I wish people would have said or done differently to help me during my grief. For as much as I didn't want to talk about it initially, I would have liked people to tell me that they were thinking of me, and that their hearts went out to me. When I returned to work, I received stone cold silence. I didn't speak to anyone except my boss on my first day back.

One coworker came over to me the next day and said, "So, are you going to ignore people like you did yesterday?" I was still in a fog, so I said, "My children just died. What do you want me to be like?"

I wish that some family members, such as my in-laws, wouldn't have avoided talking about the boys. They may have shared their love and thoughts with my husband, but around me, the topic was taboo. It was like they didn't want to upset me. But not talking about it did upset me. I later shared that with them, and they broke down crying, telling me how heartbroken they were for us, and never having lived the experience themselves, they didn't know what to say.

I wish that my husband could have opened up to me at the time or realized that an experience like this means that you need to live it and relive it. Then, and only then, can you begin to move forward. He attended one support group meeting with me but found it difficult because he had to relive it all over again.

I wish that some family members had been more supportive in their words and actions. At times, I felt people suggested that I "forget" about the babies I lost. On the day of the viewing, a relative said, "You will have more, right?"

My cousin's wife told me she hoped I "got better soon," and that next time around, she hoped I had four more. When I crafted a carefully worded response via email, she took offense and shared my response with others in the family, one of whom characterized me as "overreacting."

When my sister was pregnant, it was also difficult. She was insulted that I tried to keep my distance to protect myself emotionally. She told me that when our father had died, she decided she had to stop feeling so sad, and she couldn't understand why I wasn't doing the same. Her words, "It wasn't like your loss happened yesterday, or even a year ago," hurt deeply. I will never forget those words and how they sliced my wounds open again.

We now have two daughters. Kaelin was born March 10, 2009, exactly two years to the day after my sons' funeral and when we said our final goodbyes. I believe that my sons sent Kaelin to us so that we could experience more sunshine than pain in the month of March. Our second daughter, Kelsey, was a complete surprise, born in

September, 2011. We are expecting a son due September 2019

Our first year, and in subsequent years, we released balloons at the beach for them—balloons onto which we had written messages. Now the girls and I have done a balloon release at the cemetery, as well as place flowers on their grave.

The way I deal with my grief is by being the best mom that I can to my rainbow babies. They are my reason for living. I immersed myself in the March of Dimes. I started a walk team in 2008, which we have continued each year since. I serve on several March of Dimes committees. We were also the Pittsburgh March of Dimes Ambassador Family in 2014. I have been a volunteer with the March of Dimes Share Your Story site. Those activities keep me going, give me purpose, and allow me to do good things in my sons' memory.

The experience of losing Ethan and Casey has made me realize what is important in this life. It has made me tell others how much I love them while they are still on this earth. All too often, we share our best thoughts and feelings about people after they are gone.

I am more patient with my kids, and I try to appreciate all the ups and downs that go with parenthood. I try to live my life in a way that my sons would be proud.

REMEMBERING BABY DEAN,
as told by his mother Michelle

"I have so many regrets. I regret that we didn't hold him, bury him, see him. We did nothing. No one told us we should do all those things."

Dean Allan was born on January 11, 2000—lost at twenty-one weeks' gestation. I went in for my ultrasound on January 6 and we were called in to our OB the following day. We were told Dean had developed a cystic hygroma (a tumor on his neck). It usually doesn't show up till the third trimester and most children who live with this don't make it past one year old.

We wanted a second opinion, so we went to a specialist at West Penn Hospital in Pittsburgh. They could not find a heartbeat when we arrived. He had developed fetal hydrops, a condition which a baby cannot survive. I was too far along for a D&C, so we were told the delivery would need to be induced. I was taken to the labor and delivery room to start the process and eighteen hours later, I delivered Dean.

I have so many regrets.

I regret that we didn't hold him, see him, bury him. We did nothing. No one told us we should do all those things. The hospital staff did take pictures of Dean, yet they didn't give them to us. When I called back looking to obtain the photos, I was told they couldn't find them.

I wish we would have chosen to go home and prepared a bit better. I wish I would have held our son and taken care of him properly. I regret this every day of my life.

I've have asked Dean to forgive us for not knowing—for not realizing what we were doing. I was so overwhelmed.

My grief journey has been a process for more than eighteen years. We had tried so hard to have a baby and I believe I was grieving the loss of my son as well as my loss of not being able to get pregnant.

I always think of "what if" and I don't know if that ever goes away.

Initially, I was in shock. Everything happened so fast with finding no heartbeat, being taken straight to a labor and delivery room to begin the long hours of inducing me. I could barely speak to anyone and have no idea who visited me during that period. While I was still carrying Dean and before we knew he was gone, our church gathered around us, anointed us and prayed with us. Following his death, my husband and I, along with our pastor, had a small Scripture reading and prayer time for him. I struggle to this day about how we handled the time in the hospital.

All these years later, I now reflect on the anniversary date of my son's birth as a way to honor Dean and find peace in how my life has been. I know that my life is the way God wanted it to be and I try to stay focused on that.

At the time, I had no support. I was expected to move on. I had to come to terms with the fact that I was pregnant once and never again.

There were no support groups, and family and friends didn't know how to deal with me. I really felt I couldn't talk about Dean, I didn't have a right to honor him publicly. My husband was somewhat supportive in the first few years.

I felt so empty and I went into such a deep depression. When no one ever acknowledged Dean, it made it all the worse. People would tell me years later that they didn't want to make me sad by bringing him up. Why I felt that I needed to stay silent is something I'll never know. I just wish that someone, anyone would have asked:

"How are you feeling?"

"Do you want to talk about your loss?"

"May I do something to remember your baby?"

Anything at all would have helped. I was told to move on (in a birthday card), four months after my loss.

We spent another three years trying to conceive with infertility drugs, IUI (intrauterine insemination) and IVF's. I had finally decided it was time for me to grieve not being able to get pregnant and have my own child. Once I decided to do that, we began our adoption journey and adopted a baby boy.

Today, I don't take any pregnancy for granted in any circumstance. I cherish the birth of a newborn because I know that anything can happen. I feel strongly about every child having a chance at life.

JOURNAL PROMPT

Was there anything specific that you wish people would have said or done, but didn't, that would have helped you during your grief?

CHAPTER 5

ECHOES OF OTHERS WHO HAVE WALKED THE SAME PATH: YOU'RE NOT ALONE.

Years down the road on your journey of grief, out of nowhere, you may find yourself in a situation where you hear of a young mother who recently lost an infant. The news tugs at your heart as you nod with understanding.

The instinct to share your experience, even if sometimes in a whisper by saying, "I lost a baby, too—it was a long time ago," comes rushing to the surface and you instantly feel connected. Bereaved mothers and fathers have a common bond.

REMEMBERING MEGHAN MARIE,
as told by her mother, Maureen

"Looking back, I wish that people would not have acted like there was an elephant in the room. I didn't care if they asked me questions—I wanted to be able to talk about my feelings."

Meghan Marie was born on November 11, 1978. She passed away on October 12, 1979, just one month shy of her first birthday, having never come home from the hospitals where she was cared for.

As a young, twenty-four-year-old newlywed, Maureen and her husband, Jim, were living in Ohio when she unexpectedly went into labor with their firstborn on that day that she had intended to take a trip to Pittsburgh to visit family. Instead, Maureen was rushed to the local hospital emergency room where she delivered a tiny baby girl who weighed just two pounds, twelve ounces.

Baby Meghan was immediately transferred to a hospital in West Virginia that was equipped to care for a premature baby. Maureen did not get to see her newborn for several days until she, herself, was released from the hospital, but her husband made sure that the baby was baptized. A male nurse who accompanied Meghan on the transport became her stand-in Godfather.

Forty years later, Maureen can recall the time of Meghan's birth as if it were recent.

"The first few days were so difficult as I couldn't see her and I did not think she was going to survive. Meghan was taken in her bassinet and transferred, and I had only gotten to see her for a few minutes. My mother came to stay with me and she was a source of support and help, but after some time, she also had to get back home to her family. I made the thirty-minute drive to the hospital every single day. And every evening, Jim and I would go back. I was a new mother and spent almost all of my time alone at the hospital.

"I remember that when I did finally see Meghan for the first time, she was off the ventilator but I was totally shocked. Her skin was so transparent—it was very scary. She looked like a little baby doll lying in the bassinet at barely three pounds and she was only 15.5 inches long. She was attached to a heart monitor and oxygen, and had tiny patches covering her eyes. It was probably another month until I was allowed to hold her."

The journey was long and days turned into months.

"There were many incidents that happened while Meghan spent months in the hospital. Jim and I never wanted to rock the boat with those who were caring for our child. We were young parents and inexperienced. One time the hospital staff gave Meghan a little too much morphine. One time they forgot to mark that she was fed when she had been. There was also another time she had been moved to a regular room with a regular bed. They had mixed up Meghan with another patient. They even had a toothbrush and gown there—they didn't know she was a baby. I did speak up then. I asked why she was moved and they said it was hospital rules. They never had a baby in for so long. They didn't know what to do with her, so they put her into an adult room, an adult bed. How horrible to see a tiny baby in such a big hospital bed."

By the following May, Jim's job transferred the couple back to Pittsburgh. Meghan was flown by an air ambulance and transported to Magee Women's Hospital where she remained under special care for the next five months. She would never come home.

Meghan died on Friday, October 12, 1979. She was honored at a memorial service and buried at the nearby cemetery in a special section for infants. Maureen was amazed at the number of people who came to pay their respects on that chilly day in October.

Family and friends quickly came together in support. On Saturday, a close friend, who was a priest, presided over a funeral service for Meghan. The grandmothers came and brought her a little outfit to be buried in. Maureen and Jim thought it would be a private service with just family, but there were more than fifty people at the cemetery—all who had gathered and come together in less than twenty-four hours.

Maureen did not know until years later how the funeral director had transported her baby Meghan from the funeral home. She was devastated to hear from others that he came to the cemetery and opened the trunk of his car to take out the casket. No one said anything of the haunting and insensitive act, but everyone wondered why he could not have placed the infant's casket on the front or back seat. Maureen could not shake the horrible image and was exasperated.

The outpouring of emotions and sympathy was a comfort to Maureen and Jim as the young couple grieved together. She remembered a cousin who was always the life of every party who could not even speak—he left the funeral service so distraught with no words to say.

At the time, Maureen didn't know anyone who had lost a baby, and as far as professional support went, there was none. They relied on family and friends.

Maureen always felt blessed that Jim was a very supportive husband and she credits him for providing the strength she needed to endure the loss of their firstborn.

There were times when he'd be overwhelmed—going to work, traveling, going to our home without our baby, a year of going to hospitals. There were days when it really got to him. Yet on the day that Meghan died, he could not cry. Jim felt that he had to be strong for Maureen and did not want her to see him break down.

"I remember my own father took Jim for a walk one day and he said to him, 'Your dad is ill and unable to give you fatherly advice right now, but I'm going to tell you that you have to show your emotions.'"

Those were important words from one father to another.

Soon after Meghan died, the young couple received flowers from everyone they knew. When a delivery came from old neighbors, Jim was moved to tears realizing the support of others. Donations were taken and one man only had five dollars, but promised to give more on payday and he followed up later by sending more money. Jim and Maureen were very moved by the all of the acts of kindness for their loss.

Every year Jim sends Maureen flowers on the anniversary of Meghan's death—now it has been forty years. Through all of life's busy schedules and craziness, Jim never forgot the day that his first daughter died.

"No one ever told me to forget about my loss, but someone once asked me why I had a picture of her displayed in my home, and that hurt me deeply. Why not? Meghan was part of our family and always will be, even if she was not alive. Don't we display photographs of our grandparents or other relatives who are deceased? Looking back, I wish that people would not have acted like there was an elephant in the room. I didn't care if they asked me questions—I wanted to be able to talk about my feelings. I remember that I attended a baby shower after Meghan died and everyone tried to shield me. I really didn't want that."

After losing Meghan, Jim's job transferred the couple to Kentucky for several years and they had a daughter, Erin, followed by a son, Brendan.

"The experience of losing Meghan as an infant changed me to realize how precious life is and how it can be taken in a minute. I remember being pregnant with my daughter, Erin. I was so nervous and so afraid. I kept thinking I can't go through this again.

"The loss also made me scared to death with my other pregnancies and I think it made me an over-protective mother. Later, I went on to have a career of twenty-four years working with special needs children. I couldn't help but think that had she survived, Meghan would have faced a life of challenges, just like the children I worked with.

"In my journey, I often think of Meghan, especially when I see her cousins of the same age reaching different milestones in their lives. When our daughter got married and had a baby, she asked if it would be okay if they named their daughter Meghan. She asked if I would mind and I told her that I would be honored. It was bittersweet and also heartwarming.

"Our story came full circle when we moved back to Pittsburgh in 1985. I met a neighbor who had suffered a miscarriage and later had another baby who died at only a few days old. We shared stories and she mentioned a doctor from the hospital—Dr. Robert Cicco. I couldn't believe that it was the same man who was Meghan's doctor when she was being cared for at that hospital. I had not seen him since she passed away in 1979—six years earlier. I clearly remember the day Meghan died. Dr. Cicco was not working, but he came in when he heard the news.

"I made an appointment at his pediatric office and took my children there. When Dr. Cicco came into the office, he instantly recognized me and said, "Maureen, how are you? I haven't seen you in so long." It warmed my heart that he remembered me. He told me about a transitional infant care (TIC) hospital that had been started in Pittsburgh as a place to care for medically-fragile infants that had spent lengthy time in a hospital. The seeds had been planted during Dr. Cicco's fellowship when he cared for Meghan and observed the impact that caring for a sick child had on families.

"I had wondered all those years 'Why did Meghan die? What was the reason?'

"I had to move out of town and back, out of town and back. I now know that the doctor's mind started thinking of the idea and realizing the need for a transitional center or home for infants, after treating and caring for Meghan for so long back in 1979. Originally known as the Transitional Infant Care Home, it is now The Children's Home of Pittsburgh Lemieux Family Center.

"Learning this made me think back to a family member saying, 'You may not realize now, but everyone is put on this earth to do one job. And when their job is done, they get their reward and go to Heaven. Whether they get a minute, an hour, a day, or one hundred years, when they get that job done, they go to Heaven.'

"Back then, it never clicked. But now it all clicks. We feel that is why Meghan was here. Some people may never know, but sometimes it just goes full circle.

"If only I would have had a book like this when I lost Meghan, I would not have felt so alone by myself. I hope that telling my story and remembering Meghan might help someone else going through the worst time of their life due to infant loss."

REMEMBERING BABY ROBERT,
as told by his mother, Colleen

"I can still remember his face. I can close my eyes forty-eight years later and still see his beautiful face."

I read your article in the *Pittsburgh Post-Gazette* today and was touched to learn that there is help for mothers that are grieving for their babies from a miscarriage or death. It was very emotional. I remembered so many details that I guess a mother never forgets. Support was something that I only wish was available to me when I needed help.

I had both a miscarriage and a son that died two days after birth. The miscarriage happened in 1968 and the death of my son was June 5, 1969. My son was named Robert James and he was born June 3, 1969. He lived for only two days. He was premature by six weeks. He weighed five pounds, six ounces and was twenty inches long. At first we were told everything was fine and then we were told that there was a problem with his lungs. I only saw him for a minute after he was born and I can still remember his face. I have his birth record with his footprint as the only memory of him. I can close my eyes forty-eight years later and still see his beautiful face.

I cried to read the newspaper article and reflected on Robert, even after all these years have passed. Married at eighteen, I was only twenty-one when I lost my firstborn.

I can still clearly remember going back to my OB-GYN's office for my six-week check-up after losing Baby Robert. The attending physician asked me if I was nursing my baby. (He obviously did not read my records or remember my case.) I had to remind him that my baby died.

You think nobody cares. Although I must say that my husband was always my strongest support. After all these years of carrying that loss, when he recently died, I told him it was time to go ahead and be with our son.

I would consider it an honor to share my story. I feel that young bereaved mothers would benefit by knowing that others have gone through the same heartache as they are experiencing, and that perhaps, this might give them some comfort. Thank you for the work you are doing to help mothers who are going through this pain.

--Colleen

REMEMBERING BABY AMY MICHELLE,
as told by her mother, Carol

"This loss became a great blow to our entire family. Granted, I had two beautiful healthy babies but I was still mourning my third baby."

Your feature in the *Pittsburgh Post-Gazette* really hit home for me. In 1979, I was pregnant with triplets. I had been trying to get pregnant for four years, attended Resolve meetings, and even applied for adoption. We were then blessed to find out we were pregnant. At twenty weeks we found out I was carrying triplets! We were very happy and yet very scared.

The first words out of my husband's mouth after that sonogram were, "What if they all want to go to medical school?"

It was an easy pregnancy. I worked until thirty-three weeks when I became pre-eclamptic. My OB-GYN told me to go to the hospital for some blood work and, little did I know, they were admitting me to labor and delivery. Triplet pregnancies were not as common then and they put me in the Maternal Fetal ICU every time I had a contraction. The NICU team was always on call and three isolettes were always ready. Once when the ICU was full, I was in a labor room and was given magnesium sulfate for my blood pressure. The medication either went in too fast or was too much, and my blood pressure dropped severely.

My husband was sleeping in the chair beside me, but I couldn't speak. I had an out-of-body experience in which I was above in the corner of the room and saw many people come in and running around, and someone said to turn off the IV. After that, I started to feel warm and came back.

The staff had difficulty getting the fetal heart tones for a while, but told me it was the position of the babies. Baby A's heart rate started to decline and I had an emergency C-section. I was thirty-five weeks. My husband was not allowed in the OR, since it was an emergency, and he was very upset.

Our babies were born on October 9, 1979.

Baby A was a girl and weighed four pounds, four ounces.

Baby B was a boy and weighed four pounds, six ounces.

Baby C was a girl and only weighed two pounds, eight ounces. She was a stillborn and had not grown well since her location was at the top of my uterus. They feel she had died about two weeks prior to delivery, yet no one ever mentioned this to me.

We named our baby girl Amy Michelle.

I had been given a triplet baby shower. My father had made three wooden cradles and was designing a birth announcement for triplets. This loss became a great blow to our entire family. Granted, I had two beautiful healthy babies but I was still mourning my third baby.

I really wanted to see our baby, Amy, and the nurses were against this. I had to ask the night supervisor to help by going to the morgue so that I could see her. I really needed this for closure.

I then had to make arrangements to have Amy buried with no guidance from anyone. My father-in-law suggested that we have Amy buried with my husband's grandmother who had recently passed away, and that is what we did.

I became very ill with a fever after the delivery and could not attend the funeral service. I went home two weeks after I delivered and became very busy with our two surviving babies. I was very exhausted.

At times, it was suggested that I try to "forget" about the baby I lost, and was reminded that I had two healthy babies. I never really had time to grieve, but I did have a very supportive family.

Thanks very much for the opportunity to share my story. This is a very important subject that needs to be brought out into the open. I became more sensitive to others in the same circumstance and maybe it will help others feel the same.

Sincerely,
Carol

Remembering Baby Walter Scott,
as told by his mother, Kathie, to her daughter, Stephanie

"The staff never even showed the baby to my mother. She was moved to a regular room and remembers my father coming into the room with a baby-blue elephant planter. She never saw the baby the rest of the day and kept busy writing out baby announcements that said "Baby from Heaven!"

 This is my mom's story about losing her son, Walter Scott, who was born April 25 and died April 26, 1968. She was twenty-four at the time. This was her second pregnancy and was induced two weeks early at Magee Women's Hospital, Pittsburgh. Her actual due date was Mother's Day.

My mother never had morning sickness and considered it to be an easy pregnancy. There were no signs of any problems at all, but these were the days before sonograms. The circumference of the baby's head was normal and she had carried him well, although he was much smaller than her first baby, a girl born two years earlier.

Baby Walter was born at 12:04 p.m., weighing five pounds, eleven ounces and 19½ inches long. He had brown hair and blue eyes. He was born quickly, before my mother was in the delivery room. He cried out and the umbilical cord was cut, but she and my father were never told that there was a problem with his breathing.

The staff never even showed the baby to my mother. She was moved to a regular room and remembers my father coming into the room with a baby blue elephant planter. She never saw the baby the rest of the day and kept busy writing out baby announcements that said "Baby from Heaven!"

When my mother's sister came to visit, the nurse held the baby up in the nursery for her to see and she saw that he was on oxygen. When she went in to see my mother, she asked if she knew the baby was on oxygen.

My mother has no recollection of ever holding Walter Scott, but in his baby book she wrote that she saw him three times. Mom thinks that maybe she went down to the nursery after she learned about the oxygen.

The following morning, my mother heard nurses bringing the babies to the new moms and she asked where her baby was and was told to go back to the room while they were doing tests on Baby Walter. The nurses did not know if anything was wrong with him as they waited to get a hold of the pediatrician. Later, various doctors began coming in and asking my mother about family heart condition history. Next, a nurse said they had to call my father and get him to the hospital.

Things happened quickly. A hospital chaplain came and said that they had to decide on a name and baptize the baby. My parents were not present, only a nurse was witness to the baptism.

Baby Walter was then transported by a taxi cab in his incubator with a nurse to Pittsburgh Children's Hospital. My father followed the baby in his car to the hospital.

Baby Walter died near nine that night.

My father donated the baby's eyes to the eye bank and never told Mom until later that summer.

An autopsy was performed and determined the cause of death to be hyaline membrane disease, or immature lungs. No paperwork or documentation was ever provided.

My father took Mom home from the hospital the next day, though she should have stayed. He had already placed the cradle in the attic and put away all the baby items. It was decided for Baby Walter Scott to be buried next to his grandfather. Only my father and my mother's parents went to the cemetery.

My father never talked about Baby Walter Scott again.

Kathie and Walt had two daughters born in 1969 and 1972. Decades later, they also had four grandsons between 1994 and 2008. The fourth grandson was born April 26, 2008, at 12:05 p.m., sharing the same date when his uncle, Walter Scott's short life ended forty years earlier.

JOURNAL PROMPT

Prior to your own loss, did you personally know anyone who lost a baby, and how did it affect you? Did it help to hear how others coped with their loss?

CHAPTER 6

LETTERS FROM INTERNATIONAL BEREAVED MOTHER'S DAY

The following letters were sent to author, Joann Cantrell, in response to a *Pittsburgh Post-Gazette* feature published on International Bereaved Mother's Day, April 2017, and several previous first-person essays published on infant loss.

I wrote three separate features on infant loss for the *Pittsburgh Post-Gazette*, in 2002, 2009 and 2017. Each time, I received such an outpouring of compelling stories from readers, and each response and interview took careful thought, attention, and time. Despite the span of years in between features, what remained consistent was the desperate feelings of emptiness and loneliness for the bereaved parents who had lost an infant.

Forgive my familiarity, but we share something in common and I've been meaning to write since first reading "The Cruelest Season," now more than seven months ago. The article touched such a chord of understanding in me, that I had to write and tell you that you captured what I've been feeling myself. Oddly enough, today would have been the sixth birthday of my daughter who consequently died of complications sustained during birth. How suddenly we went from "high fives" in the birthing suite to flying down the hall to an emergency delivery. Thus, the cruelest season for me begins with the Advent season and all the preparations of such a joyous season. Bittersweet, heart wrenching, and draining.

Thank you for touching all of us who have lost children and always hesitate and swallow hard when asked how many children we have. And, for reminding us that we're not alone when we're always so aware of the one who is missing.

Peace,
Joan

I wanted to let you know how much your feature impacted me and how beautifully written it was. I know that writing from the heart is always powerful and your piece spoke to me on so many levels. I am the mother of a stillborn son. He was born and buried in November 1999. I still carry him with me and know that I always will. Unless someone has lived with the pain of burying a child, they cannot comprehend it. I cried with you when I read your article.

I worked for Newborns in Need, a nonprofit organization that helped babies in crisis. The outreach included many facets, especially in some of the lower income areas in Southwestern Pennsylvania. We donate regularly to many hospitals and facilities including newborn layettes and preemie items. We make items for the tiniest babies when items cannot be purchased. Sadly, we also donate burial layettes for babies who have passed away. Each burial layette includes a gown, hat, booties and a blanket.

I realize that the small gift we give to each family has an impact much stronger than we could ever imagine. Thank you for opening my eyes and giving me the understanding that what we do is so very important. Since I was never the recipient of this type of kindness, I did not understand the impact that it could have on the families that we serve. It has renewed my efforts and lifts my spirits when our mission struggles.

--Leticia

Fifty years ago on September 4, 1967, my well-controlled, well-planned, gently protected, and faith-filled life was shaken to its very core. I found my firstborn child—a beautiful, healthy, two-month-old baby girl—dead in her crib. At first, the shock was numbing, but then came the pain, the anger, the Why's? I clung to my faith reflexively and almost like insurance, because I knew that it was my only hope of being reunited with my child. God and I had many anguished conversations and I would weep, crying out to God. I quietly cried through many church services, but I would always keep my eyes focused on a bright red cross that hung on the back wall of our church. Often, after times when I was most emotional, a sense of peace and comfort would come and I felt as if

God would wrap me in His arms and gently let me know that He was in control.

--Grace

After reading your article, "Forever in Our Hearts," I just want to say thank you for putting into words how I often feel. Your story resonates with me as I recently lost my twins, Bryce James and Ava Priscilla, shortly after their birth.

--Anna

Thank you for sharing your story—I REALLY needed to hear it today. My son's due date is April 6th and like your twins, he was born too early at five months into the pregnancy. I am struggling this week with feelings of emptiness and it helped me a lot to remember that there are others out there who feel the same as I do. God Bless.

--Lisa

I know the pain you are going through every day. I have lost four babies. I am so sorry for your loss. We all have to take it day by day, and sometimes, hour by hour.

I am here to listen and give support. Maybe we, as bereaved mothers, can support each other through our grief.

--Loretta

Your article touched my heart as no other has. My baby died April 28, 1960, decades ago, and the pain is still there. We had five other children, yet the loss of Gary was devastating. I live with the loss, but know that no one understands why it still hurts. No one, except for my husband, that is. I think I can talk about it, but inevitably, the tears come. Thank you for the article. You said so much, so well. I will save the article.

With love and prayers,
Gerry

My heart ached for you as I read your article. I, too, lost a child when I was six months pregnant. Our daughter, Kayleigh, was stillborn on July 21, 1999. It was so unexpected that it still has an unreal quality about it. I had been dreaming of having a little girl since I was sixteen. I couldn't understand what I had done that God would take her away.

I played the "what if" game endlessly and thought I did everything right. Part of me still blames myself.

When I became pregnant with our son, I had no idea how to answer the question, "Is this your first child?" We now have two beautiful boys and I still hesitate when asked, "How many children do you have?" or "Are you going to try for a girl?"

When I lost her, I just wanted to tell people about her—to say her name, to have someone acknowledge that I was a mother, even though I didn't have my child. Unfortunately, some people were too uncomfortable and I learned to clam up.

Fortunately, I did find a support system. I worked in a doctor's office and my boss and his wife, patients, friends, and even strangers who learned of my loss, would come up to me and tell me of children they had lost. Hearing their stories, I couldn't believe that some of these women could still get out of bed in the morning. It helped me deal with Kayleigh's death, thinking that if others could get through it, so could I.

Time does not heal all wounds but I have gotten better at coping. "That which does not kill us only makes us stronger."

I can think of Kayleigh now and smile. I still think of her every day and I wonder what it would have been like to raise her. I have her framed footprints on the mantle between her brothers' pictures and I take comfort in that.

--Kristen

I remember after my miscarriage, my brother said, "You're strong, you'll be okay." I didn't feel very strong that day. People, in an attempt to comfort one another, often say things that aren't very comforting. I remember driving to the hospital the day I miscarried, and all the leaves were starting to come out and the grass was so green. Everything was waking up and coming to life, and I thought, "Everything belongs to the Lord. It is His to give and His to take away. His ways are not our ways." We can never understand why some things happen, but that is where faith comes in.

--Lori

A friend emailed me your story. I, too, lost my son, Benjamin, in April 2000, and I wanted to let you know how much I appreciated your article. It meant a lot to see a bereaved mother's thoughts in print. I am sorry for the loss of your boys and glad that you found someone so special to care for them so far away.

--Karen

Like your twins, my daughter Julia died at thirty-nine-and-a-half weeks and was stillborn in 1999. I now write a newsletter for a bereavement group that I faithfully attend each month and I look for inspirational stories. We are a small bereavement group that began more than twenty years ago by a woman who lost her son at birth. Our newsletter reaches approximately two hundred people who have been touched by the HOPE group, affiliated with

Winchester Hospital in Winchester, Mass, twenty miles northwest of Boston. (The HOPE Group offers support for bereaved individuals and families who have experienced a miscarriage, stillbirth or neonatal death.)

Your analogy of the crocuses being capable of surviving the harshest conditions and how it relates to you (as a bereaved mother) after your twins' death, is touching. I can so relate to surviving the harshest conditions immediately following Julia's death as well as the many holidays and family gatherings without her. Your words give me hope and strength to remember Julia as the springtime and good weather approaches.

--Donna

Thank you for writing your article in the *Pittsburgh Post-Gazette* on what it is like to be a mom who has had a baby die. I was so happy to see the article among all of the other Mother's Day pieces because it shows everyone that we are here on this day, too, and the day can be painful. I hope it inspires friends and family members not to forget the bereaved moms whose children are in heaven.

I gave birth to premature quads in the month of March and they all died. Like you, spring and blooming of the spring flowers through the snow will be bittersweet for me. I hated seeing daffodils coming up. I am lucky in that I found an incredibly wonderful group of women through an online forum on infant loss and we share our experiences. They are the same experiences you wrote about and have shared with readers. We have been struggling with Mother's Day and this article struck home.

Thank you for sharing your experience.

--Margie

Hooray—an article for us! Among all the ads and articles for Mother's Day, the *Pittsburgh Post-Gazette* published an article for bereaved mothers, "The Cruelest Season." I can't thank the author and newspaper enough for including a feature that recognizes our existence as Mother's Day approaches.

--Marie

Thank you for posting this article. I have actually printed it. It almost amazes me that we can read an article written by someone we don't know who isn't part of our support group, yet says all of the same things that we seem to share—the same words and feelings. Whenever I read things such as this, I sit back and say, "See, it is not just me. I am not being dramatic about this. These feelings are so real and it makes me realize that it's okay for me not to let go. It's true, while thinking that being close to someone else who had twins would rip my heart out in a million different directions, I know that I can survive the harshest conditions, too.

--Helen

Thank you for writing this article. So many mothers feel down with Mother's Day. This has given them encouragement to know that someone has spoken out for them.

I think that is why I am feeling so rotten at the moment—because of Mother's Day, and I know I will not be acknowledged…I just know it. I cannot wait for the day to be over. I would also like to thank the newspaper, the *Pittsburgh Post-Gazette*. It is nice to know that they did recognize that we do exist.

--Crystal

JOURNAL PROMPT

What would you like to say about your baby? This can be a love letter to your child or to someone else, telling them about your child.

CHAPTER 7

PERSPECTIVES FROM FATHERS

THIS MORNING
by Al Andrews

I wash the face of their gravestone
bowing to the task anxious
as if my children
could see the sweat glistening on my face
the rag swishing the white granite
my hands tugging at tiny weeds
around the stone
I don't come here often
and never linger
the wind blows too lonely
and the sun never warms

A LETTER REMEMBERING BABY BETH AND JEFF,
from their father, Al

"Even though the deaths of two of our three children happened fifty years ago, the memories are always with us. Looking back, we are proud of the way we have handled their deaths and are willing and able to share it with others in need…rightly or wrongly, our thoughts were that we didn't want to hear that Beth and Jeff had died because God wanted another angel."

Your excellent article has inspired me to let you know of the heartache suffered by my wife, Rosanne, and me after the deaths of our two beloved children, Beth and Jeff, back in the 1960s.

Rosanne and I were with our four-year-old son, Jim, and our infant daughter, Beth, at a visit with our family pediatrician. It was a follow-up appointment shortly after Beth had been hospitalized in Camden, New Jersey, where she had been treated for severe vomiting and dehydration. The doctors could not find what caused Baby Beth to be so sick.

The young pediatrician examined Beth and measured the circumference of her head. He looked at us and told us to cancel a trip we had planned to New York. He had discovered that Beth's head was growing larger—an indication of a very serious problem with her brain.

He had called St. Christopher's Children's Hospital in Philadelphia and told us to get her there immediately.

At the hospital, we waited anxiously as Beth was being examined, and I overheard two nurses talking.

"My God," I heard the one nurse say. "They have already lost another child."

96

She had obviously read the file of our family medical history that recounted the story of our oldest child, Jeff, who had died at two-and-a-half years old when he was hit by a delivery truck coming out of a blind alley and onto the sidewalk where little Jeff was walking.

Beth was diagnosed with encephalitis, and she was in the hospital for over a week. The doctors inserted a shunt in her head to drain the excess fluid from her brain. We were allowed to take her home, and she seemed to rally. Her sweet smile gave us hope; however, she quickly started to slip downhill and was re-admitted to St. Christopher's. She was then sent to Temple University's Oncology Unit for more invasive tests. It tore us apart to see our dear baby girl suffer.

Back at St. Christopher's, the pediatric brain surgeon said they thought she had a brain tumor and that they would have to operate on her immediately. The surgeon, whom we had gotten to know quite well, told us that they were going to perform the operation later that night. He recommended that we go home with Jim and said he would call us when the operation was over.

That night never seemed to end. Rosanne slept while I sat next to the bed staring at the green phone on the nightstand. Was it ever going to ring? As dawn was breaking, the phone rang, I picked it up and heard the surgeon's heart-breaking words, "I'm sorry."

Even though the deaths of two of our three children happened fifty years ago, the memories are always with us. Looking back, we are proud of the way we have handled their deaths and are willing and able to share it with others in need. We never did join any therapy groups. At the time, we were moving around the country with my various corporate jobs and, rightly or wrongly, our thoughts were that we didn't want to hear that Beth and Jeff had died because "God wanted another angel."

We are a successful, well-rounded, and well-traveled couple now in our seventies. Our only living son is now in his fifties, was an honor graduate of Northwestern University, and has been successful in business. After Beth's death, Rosanne and I decided to live our lives to the fullest and dedicate ourselves to helping individuals and organizations who could use our help—be it money, time, or effort.

We are all the better for it.

May God bless you, and may this book bring comfort and some peace to people who certainly deserve to have it.

A LETTER REMEMBERING
BABY WILLIAM JOSEPH
from his father, Tom

"Every day as I work in the yard, I can see my son's marker, which always serves as a reminder of the son we lost and the funeral he did not have."

 My name is Tom, and I was particularly touched when reading about your loss and the funeral arrangements made for your twin sons. Back in 1960, my wife and I lost a son, William Joseph, who only lived three days because of a heart deformity. Reading your story brought tears to my eyes because what we did was unconscionable. We were young and inexperienced, and through ignorance, we listened to someone on the nursing staff who suggested that we let a funeral director handle everything. There was a burial with no blessing, no graveside service, or anything.

We have since read and heard of other infant deaths where funeral and memorial services were held. Our very own grandson, born in 1998, also survived for only three days. He was born with a liver problem. He had a funeral service with everyone participating and singing "Amazing Grace." This made us feel even more guilt-ridden over not having a memorial for our son.

We did have a flat grave marker installed for our little fella, and it was in place for many years until we replaced it with a new upright one recently. We took the original flat marker and placed it in our backyard. To an outsider, it may seem "tacky," but every day as I work in the yard, I can see my son's marker, which always serves as a reminder of the son we had lost and the funeral he did not have. I don't want to appear maudlin, but my eyes are welling up as I send this note.

Even though we have six other sons (two sets of twins), William Joseph will live in our hearts forever.

Respectfully yours,
Tom

REMEMBERING BABY ASHLYN MARIE,
as told by her father, Andrew

"One in a thousand, they tell us. One in a thousand—like it's supposed to make you feel better. You never think that one is going to be you. It's always someone else. Until it happens. You're the one."

 Andrew Yackuboskey had just turned thirty-three in May 2016, when he graduated from Penn State and received his second degree, an

Associate's in Mining Engineering. He was determined to get straight A's, and with a friendly, competitive goal to do better than his uncle who had graduated before him. Being extremely focused, Andrew's hard work paid off as he completed his degree with a 3.97 GPA (grade point average).

A month later, on June 20, 2016, Andrew and his wife, April, were changed forever when their daughter, Ashlyn, was stillborn at thirty-nine weeks. In an instant, nothing of what he had focused on before mattered—none of it.

Andrew began writing journal entries in the days and months that followed, trying to make sense of his deep love for the daughter he lost and his struggle as a young, grief-stricken father. Ashlyn's journal became a tender, intimate expression from a male perspective of his raw emotions and experiences that he faced without Ashlyn. The journal entries were published in 2018 exactly as they were written. The book traces Andrew's journey in dealing with the overwhelming devastation and raw grief, while nurturing a deeper faith in God and hope for healing.

A journal entry from *Ashlyn's Journal* by Andrew Yackuboskey:

There are no breaks (for us) only suffering. When I forget the "feeling" of her, that'll be another deathblow to me. It will be like losing her all over again. I hope that day does not come soon.

When the routine of life reaches me, that will be another gut shot as well. It will be like closing one chapter in my life that I desperately want to keep open, in the hopes that she'll return, and this has been just a horrible nightmare, I'll wake up one day and start a whole new chapter without her and realize she's gone, because she's not in it (and she's never coming back). That'll be like losing her all over again, too.

I don't know what it's like to be a stillbirth mother…I do know what it's like to be a stillbirth father—to feel useless and helpless to save the ones you love the most. I know what that feels like. Healing can only begin through remembering your child and forgiving yourself.

JOURNAL PROMPT

Infant loss affects fathers in different ways, but that does not mean that he does not grieve. How can you can reach out or support a bereaved father?

CHAPTER 8

HELPING OTHERS THROUGH REMEMBERING

"I've learned that losing someone or something we love can remind us not only how fragile and temporary life is, but also how important it is to appreciate what we do have: life, health, family, friends and loved ones. And I've learned that the difficult process of healing through loss can leave us with greater emotional strength and self-reliance, and a greater awareness of what really matters in life."

Marty Tousley, bereaved mother and grief counselor

REMEMBERING BABY
DAVID LUKE
as told by his mother, Marty

"Although this death happened nearly fifty years ago, I still feel anger that I never got to see or to hold our baby, and anger with myself because I didn't demand to do so. I simply didn't know any better. There was no such thing as grief counseling for infant loss. I wasn't even moved to another room, away from the other mothers. I remained in a room with another new mom, whose baby was brought to her regularly, every four hours, as I lay there with empty arms and a broken heart."

 My husband, Michael, and I were just out of college when we married in 1965. Less than two years later we were mourning the unexpected death of our second son, David, who succumbed to an Rh^2 incompatibility when he was barely three days old.

Our baby, David Luke, was born via C-section on May 23, 1967, after what we thought had been a normal, full-term pregnancy. He died three days later, on May 26, due to a blood disorder.

I remember awakening from the anesthetic in the recovery room, with my obstetrician standing over me. "How is the baby?" I asked, and the answer was written all over his face. "Not good," he said. He explained that due to a severe Rh incompatibility between my blood type and

---

[2] The Rh factor test is done during pregnancy to identify a woman's Rh factor. In some cases, the baby's father might need an Rh factor test, too. During pregnancy, problems can occur if the mother is Rh negative and the baby is Rh positive.

the baby's, our little son was suffering from a massive breakdown of his blood cells, causing bilirubin to accumulate in his blood, leading to severe jaundice. Treatment required the baby to be kept in an incubator in the nursery for round-the-clock phototherapy (special UV light treatments) in hopes that the jaundice would clear up, but the fear was that too much damage to his organs had happened already.

My husband and I knew from the beginning that our baby's chances for survival were slim. Over the next three days, our pediatrician took over the baby's care, stopping by my hospital room several times a day to report on his condition. The news was never positive, and since I was on bed rest following the C-section, our baby was never brought to me. And I never got to see him, much less hold him before he died.

I was desperate to know what our baby David looked like. My husband and my sister did their best to describe him to me, telling me that he looked just like his older brother, Chris, who'd just passed his first birthday. That was of great comfort to me, as I knew that when Chris was born the nurses had told me they thought he was "the most beautiful baby in the nursery."

Immediately after, I was in shock. I remember feeling numb, empty, and very, very sad. From the first moments in the recovery room, I had a strong feeling of dread, as I sensed immediately that our baby would not live. With the exception of my husband, who openly shared in my sadness and fear, everyone in my family kept assuring me that baby David would be fine. After he died, no one knew what to say to me. It seemed as if our baby's death was more of a shock to them than it was to my husband and me, since they'd been in denial from the beginning. While we had feared the worst, we talked openly about it with each other, and on some level, we expected it.

Although this death happened nearly fifty years ago, and things are done so much differently now, I still feel anger that I never got to see or to hold our baby, and anger with myself because I didn't demand to do so. I simply didn't know any better, and in those days, there was no such thing as grief counseling for infant loss, much less any special postpartum care for a mother whose baby had died.

At the time, I wasn't even moved to another room, away from the other postpartum mothers. I remained in a room with another new mom, whose baby was brought to her regularly, every four hours, as I lay there with empty arms and a broken heart.

I remember one morning when the nurse's aide came into our room and told us she needed to make up our beds "before the babies are brought in for feeding." I glared at her and snarled, "I don't HAVE a baby!" I was furious to think that she hadn't been informed that one of us was a bereaved mother whose baby had died.

With the support of my husband and our one-year-old son at home, I returned to a demanding job as a nursing instructor at our local community college, and with my own determination I carried on. That October, we fulfilled our dream of having two boys close together in age by adopting our younger son, Ben, and we became a family of four.

My mother had lost a baby, too, when I was five years old. My baby brother Timothy had been born prematurely and died shortly after birth. My parents never talked to me about that, and when my David died, we never talked about that either. If I had known then what I know now, I would have done things very differently. I'm sure my mother and

I could have shared so many feelings that never got acknowledged or expressed.

What I remember most after our baby died is the silence, not only from family members and friends, but also from my colleagues when I returned to work barely three weeks later. No one ever asked me about it, and after the first week or so, everyone acted as if nothing of much significance had happened to me.

In the first few days, I did receive some lovely condolence cards and notes, and made a point to answer each and every one of them. Writing those responses was probably the most therapeutic thing I could have done, as it served as a vehicle for me to acknowledge, express, and release what I was feeling at the time. In those days, grief counseling didn't exist, and it never occurred to me to seek outside support.

Because our baby died so soon after my C-section and I was still in the hospital, I was unable to attend his burial. My husband had to make all the arrangements and go through the very simple graveside service all by himself. I've kept every single one of the condolence cards and notes I received in a special keepsake box, so I can take them out, hold them, and re-read them whenever I feel a need. Along with our baby's birth and death certificates, they are the only evidence I have that he even existed at all.

We have kept him alive in memory with our sons and their families, and all four of our grandchildren have accompanied us to visit his grave in northern Michigan. It warms my heart that our older son and his wife named our first-born grandson David, and our younger son and his bride were married on our baby David's birthday, at St. David's Church in Davie, Florida.

Having experienced, struggled with, and come to terms with my own particular share of losses over the years,

I've come to realize that grief has taught me some of life's most valuable lessons.

My lifelong interest in the subjects of attachment, loss, grief, and healing eventually led me to a career in grief counseling. In my work with bereaved individuals, families, and groups, I have witnessed over and over again the triumph of survivors over their deepest sorrow, suffering, and pain. I have seen them experience profound moments of healing and growth, and I have learned so much about surviving and transcending grief.

REMEMBERING BABY EMERSON GRIES,
as told by his mother, Lauren

"At that moment the doctor said, "Happy Birthday," and it was a memory that I hold dear to my heart. His chances of survival were slim to none, but at that moment he was very much alive, and very much a miracle, and it was his birthday. I will always appreciate her for taking that moment to celebrate him."

"My son's name is Emerson Gries. He was born and passed on March 13, 2010, after he lived for about three hours.

"At my twenty-week routine ultrasound, the doctors noticed that my amniotic fluid was low and that Emerson's kidneys were not developing as they should due to being covered with cysts. After testing and an amnio[3], the doctors confirmed that our son had autosomal recessive polycystic kidney disease. The doctors gave us the choice

---

[3] Amniocentesis is the sampling of amniotic fluid using a hollow needle inserted into the uterus, to screen for developmental abnormalities in a fetus.

to either carry the pregnancy, knowing this was a fatal diagnosis with a very strong chance he would pass away and be born still, or I could terminate the pregnancy. My husband and I chose to carry, and Emry continued to grow and develop.

"At thirty-four weeks and two days, I went into labor naturally and he was born five pounds, fourteen ounces. He cried immediately after he was born, which shocked the doctors as they truly didn't think he would even survive the pregnancy or birth. Unfortunately, his lungs were under-developed and we had to make the decision to take him off a ventilator. Emry passed away after about three hours and it became the most amazing and saddest day of my life.

"I never imagined that losing my infant would happen to me. I was in my mid-twenties and it never crossed my mind. My mother passed away from cancer two months prior to Emerson being born, and my grandfather died a month before, as well, so grief was heavy in my heart and my family. We had three deaths in three months, all of which changed our lives.

"Just like people say you can't understand the love one feels for their child when they are born, it is the same way with grief. It's almost as if you can't understand it until you have lived through it. It is intense, overwhelming, and touches your soul.

"The OB-GYN who cared for me was on call the night I delivered Emry. She wasn't my usual doctor or even a part of the practice I went to, but she was an angel that day and a part of his story. I remember when I delivered Emry and he cried, it was almost as if everyone froze. This little baby who wasn't supposed to be alive was screaming. At that moment the doctor said, "Happy Birthday," and it was a memory that I hold dear to my heart. She knew that his chances of survival were slim to none, and she knew that I was going to be a mess emotionally and physically when he would pass. But at that moment he was very much alive and very much a miracle. Emry was our miracle and it was his birthday. I will always appreciate her for taking that moment to celebrate him. She also took time after he passed to prepare me for the future and encourage me. That helped me tremendously in the hours after he died. I hung on to her words.

"As Emry was our first child, I had never experienced birth before. So, initially, after he died, I was trying to heal physically, but the grief emotionally and physically was so awful. I took a lot of walks and needed to be in nature. I exercised, because when I felt my heart pounding, it reminded me that I wasn't dead, despite how I felt. It was awfully hard. It was as if within a few weeks, the world went back to normal, but I was still struggling along, trying to find my way, longing for a baby that I grew and loved, who wasn't there.

"The first three months after he passed were very difficult. My husband and I took a trip six weeks after his death to get away on a cruise. Onboard, we sat on a balcony in the Caribbean and just cried. There is something so therapeutic in looking at the ocean and just being alone with your thoughts, feelings, and emotions. For us, we needed it. Time passed and we had to continue on trying to piece our lives back together and reshape our future. For us, we never gave up on Emry, and although the doctors didn't think he would make it past twenty-four weeks, he proved them wrong, so I do know that they, too, were sad and heartbroken when he passed.

"Emry had red hair, light eyes, and the most angelic skin. I often dream about what he would look like now. It breaks my heart that we missed out on so many amazing adventures and experiences with him, but because of him, we live our lives differently now. My grief journey has allowed me to live my life to the fullest. The initial intense grief of my loss was so hard. I could barely eat or sleep, and I never thought I would be happy again. But, as time went on, I learned to live with my grief and carry it.

"Friends I made in the bereavement community helped guide me and my family and friends were supportive and still are. For us, that was helpful. I take opportunities, I travel, I enjoy life, and I always carry his memory with me. Because of Emry, I am a better person and also deeper in my faith. I will forever be on my grief journey, and I am okay with that. It ties me to my son.

"Emry died eight-and-a-half years ago. I still cry and long for him—I think I always will. My really bad, emotional days now are fewer. Most days, I try to use his memory to live my life to the fullest and be a better person because he never had the chance. However, when I do have emotional days, they are pretty intense, especially around the holidays, his birthday, and due date.

"Some days will be hard for the rest of my life, and I know that. If I take a minute, close my eyes, I can put myself right back in that hospital bed, and that intense pain and love will come crashing over me just like it did the day he was born and died. Personally, I hope I never lose that. The pain of losing him ties me to him. So, in a way, the sadness is part of my connection to him, and I have chosen to carry it, embrace it, and cry through it. Grief is something you have to go through, not avoid. So, I'm still on my way in my journey.

"After Emry died, my family shared that my great grandmother had lost two children. But it is strange how it was never spoken about. After Emry died, I met a lot of ladies and families in the bereavement community and through church, and it was encouraging to learn that they survived and were hopeful for the future.

"For us, there was no one in our family who lost a child immediately after birth, so finding others that truly understood was important to us. We found so much comfort and friendship in attending peer-based support groups. Those couples and families have become a huge part of our lives and like a second family to us. They shared their deepest regrets, talked about the 'what ifs', and cried right alongside us, which helped us tremendously. We all took turns carrying each other as life ran its course, and we picked one another up along the way. We built a special bond and I truly appreciate them. I also am so grateful for the friends and family who let me scream, yell, and just be angry after Emry's death. They didn't try to make me feel better but rather, let me rage. Our family and friends also supported us and still do, which is important, especially on our hardest days.

"When Emry died, we had a funeral service and even had an open casket. It was very comforting to see him and be able share him with our family and friends. Hearing that someone's baby passed away, being there, actually seeing the baby, and going to the funeral, was a way for all of us to have closure.

"Because of that, we now attend any and every pregnancy and infant loss event we can. We love to remember Emry and all the babies gone too soon. We try to raise our living children so that it is important to remember their brother and that, although it is sad, it is a part of our family story. We find great comfort in attending pregnancy and infant loss events, and I do encourage newly bereaved folks to attend them, too. Sometimes just seeing all of the families there is a reminder that you are not alone.

"Mourning the loss of our son made me aware that there were limited resources in the Pittsburgh area where we live. It blew my mind that we were going to leave the hospital, no baby, and shaken. No social worker calling to follow up, not even a place to go. My funeral home gave us the names of two support groups. That was helpful and so valuable to us.

"We made it our mission to raise awareness. In 2016, my husband and I, along with five other bereaved mothers, founded a nonprofit organization called The Still Remembered Project to help women and families in the bereavement community. We have done this in Emry's memory and that is powerful."

The Christian-based nonprofit provides bereaved families with support and encouragement for losses due to miscarriage, stillbirth, or early infant death. The organization offers hope and healing throughout all stages of the grief journey by educating and working with local medical and bereavement groups, providing remembrance keepsakes to families, holding awareness events, and hosting monthly support group meetings for bereaved mothers in the Pittsburgh area. The group gives grieving families the comfort they desperately seek.

Generous volunteers and donors have joined the effort in partnering with The Still Remembered Project by organizing events, donating materials and supplies, and helping to raise awareness of the mission to support bereaved mothers and families.

Among other projects, the group has created and donated keepsakes, including memory boxes, miscarriage care packages, and sibling bags to a variety of hospitals in the area. Each item has meaning and importance in helping to gently encourage remembrance and the honoring of a baby who will always be loved.

113

Public interest has opened the floodgates of empathy and generosity. With the support of corporations and the community, The Still Remembered Project has embraced remembering and shattering the silence associated with pregnancy and infant loss.

"I don't think that people understand the depth and trauma a couple goes through losing a child. So often, people are so uncomfortable with grief and what to say or do. Even in the professional world, bereavement leave is only a few days. Quite frankly, it's ridiculous. The world expects people to move through grief so quickly. It's not possible. I think for me, allowing me to talk about Emry and my feelings was the best thing anyone could do to help me. Many did allow me to do this, and for that I'm thankful. No one ever told us to forget about Emry or our experience.

"Though Emry was our first born, we have gone on to have three little girls and a little boy after him. We also had a miscarriage. I have struggled as my living children move through life, wondering what could have been if Emry survived. Or, I think about the little and big things in life he missed out on. As a child, I remember riding the bus to and from school, and every once-in-a-while my bus driver would have a plastic bag full of lollipops to give to us as a surprise. My girls are now to the age that they ride the bus and I will never forget when their bus driver gave them lollipops for the first time. The sheer excitement of candy at the end of a school week was a simple, yet blissful act to start their weekend off right. Smiling and yelling as they walked up the driveway with their candy in their mouths, they squealed with excitement. It breaks my heart Emry will never experience this—a lollipop from his bus driver on a Friday. The simple things and the big things— knowing I will never dance with him at his wedding or attend his graduation. Knowing that is hard and so very sad.

"Today, I am a completely different person. I appreciate the small things in life, the time I spend with my family, and I truly cherish the time I have raising my children. My heart is full of empathy, compassion, and love for people. It wasn't that I didn't have compassion before, but when I hear of someone going through a loss, or they are having a hard season in their life, I feel for them. I truly care so much about bereaved mothers and families, and strive every day to raise awareness so that we can unite to support one another in the bereavement community. Last, I have a much deeper faith in God. While I lost the innocence of being pregnant and raising kids, I know that He is with me."

REMEMBERING BABY MARTY,
as told by his mother, Mary

"The advice I would give to others that know of someone who lost a child, is that sometimes simply saying, "I'm sorry," and hugging the mother or father is all that's needed."

My son, Marty Charles, was born sleeping (stillborn) on September 2, 2014. We found out at our nineteen-week ultrasound that he did not have kidneys and would not survive.

Losing a child changes you. You are forever missing a small part of you, no matter how long you knew that child. You never fully get over it, but you learn how to live and appreciate the people that you do have. Tears came often and still do.

Though it has been more than four years since losing Marty, we still miss him every day and feel it was important for our other children to know about their brother. Talking is and was a great therapy outlet. We were never ashamed to talk about Marty and try to make talking about losing our child not so taboo. My own mother lost three children and it was always talked about in my family, so that is how I learned the importance of making our baby part of our family.

My husband, Jason, and I really leaned on each other during that time and still do. We were each other's support when we were having a bad day. Our relationship grew stronger from having to bury our child—something that neither of us ever thought we would need to do or experience in our life.

I was also supported by our family and friends. My doctor also provided guidance along the way. The funeral home directors we used were also very supportive and they made the process of burying and saying goodbye to Marty as peaceful as it could be.

I was very open about how losing Marty would be sad and awkward for some to talk about and I encouraged others to ask me any questions they had. I was also honest in how I felt comfort in talking about Marty, even though I may cry. The advice I would give to others that know of someone who lost a child, is that sometimes simply saying, "I'm sorry," and hugging the mother or father is all that's needed. Not judging someone is the most important thing. You truly don't know how they are feeling.

About three years after Marty passed, Jason and I started the Lullaby Fund. The fund was started because of our experience with losing Marty. We noticed that there was a lack of resources to assist families with paying for the funeral for their child. The Lullaby Fund assists with that—

paying for all or some of the funeral costs for families. We have reached out to hospitals and funeral homes within the area to make them aware that the fund exists. We have helped about 15 families since the inception of the foundation in 2017.

We have raised funds and received generous donations and have been fortunate to qualify for a grant through the Pittsburgh Penguins Foundation, https://www.pittsburghpenguinsfoundation.org, which has allowed us to continue to help families when they need it most.

REMEMBERING SCARLETT,
as told by her mother, Stephanie

"I have found helping others to be the best way for me to cope with our loss. I often tell people that I can no longer care for Scarlett the way I want to, so I have to care for her memory instead. And I try to do that by doing good in her name. And making sure she is never forgotten."

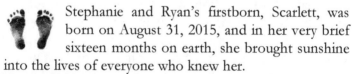 Stephanie and Ryan's firstborn, Scarlett, was born on August 31, 2015, and in her very brief sixteen months on earth, she brought sunshine into the lives of everyone who knew her.

As Stephanie shared photographs of her beautiful baby girl with a twinkle in her eyes and a smile that was like a beacon of light, the young mother described the weeks and days leading up to her death. Like every toddler, Scarlett was learning to talk, saying "MaMa" and wholeheartedly pronouncing the word "yes" when asked if she wanted a bath.

Scarlett had suffered from the usual colds and infections that were typical for toddlers her age, followed by seizures that resulted from fevers around her first birthday. She was referred to a neurologist after a third seizure in October 2016, but recovered well. Stephanie and Ryan were reassured that Scarlett's seizures were not uncommon.

On the evening of January 7, 2017, Scarlett had a low fever, and seemed fussy and more tired than usual. Still, she loved taking her bath that evening and stayed in until the water turned cold, getting upset when it was time to get out and bath time was over. Stephanie remembers how close her daughter cuddled that night, wrapped in her wearable blanket while they read their favorite book, *Barnyard Dance*.

That was the last moment they would share together as Scarlett never woke up the next morning. On Sunday, January 8, Stephanie and Ryan felt their world end when their angel Scarlett was called back to Heaven.

Their hearts, souls and lives were shattered learning that Scarlett died of Sudden Unexplained Death in Childhood (SUDC), a category of death in children between the ages of one and eighteen that remains unexplained after a thorough investigation, including an autopsy. Most often, a seemingly healthy child goes to sleep and never wakes up. At this time, it is unknown what causes SUDC, how to predict it, or how to prevent it.

"Scarlett was the light of our lives, and losing her has been the most painful experience we could ever imagine facing together," Stephanie said.

In the early weeks after losing Scarlett, the young mother's grief was very raw and her feelings continued to change almost daily. It was difficult to string together coherent thoughts, but she and Ryan did not hesitate to speak of Scarlett, her memory, or their loss to anyone who was willing to hear about her.

"Grief is not pretty, and ours certainly is not. Being able to talk about her allows me to remember she is with me always. If people don't mind seeing our grief, we don't mind showing it. We are open to mostly any opportunity to help her memory live on and we know that being a bereaved parent is a life-long struggle."

Since Scarlett's passing, Stephanie and Ryan became involved with SUDC, the only organization worldwide whose purpose is to promote awareness, advocate for research, and support families and those affected by SUDC.

SUDC is the fifth-leading category of death in children ages one to four, yet SUDC receives no public funding. The SUDC Foundation provides all services at no cost to families.

The couple has participated in several fundraisers for the Foundation and Ryan ran in the Pittsburgh Marathon as part of a team to raise money for the SUDC Foundation, raising over $11,000. They have also hosted a charity golf outing in Scarlett's memory to raise money for the SUDC Foundation on August 25th 2018, the weekend before what would have been Scarlett's third birthday. They have also established the Scarlett Lillian Pauley Foundation, which continues to raise money for the SUDC Foundation and support bereaved families in their community.

The SUDC Foundation has created a memorial website for Scarlett, sudc.org/scarlett, and Stephanie has been able to return to her work roots in communications by working for the Foundation with its public relations and communications efforts.

"I have found helping others to be the best way for me to cope with our loss," Stephanie explains. I often tell people that I can no longer care for Scarlett the way I want to, so I have to care for her memory instead. And I try to do that by doing good in her name. And making sure she is never forgotten."

Stephanie and Ryan welcomed their second child, another little girl, Eliana Scarlett, in February 2018. Being a mother again to a living child is so bittersweet, and Scarlett's absence is felt constantly. The sisters' resemblance tugs at the heart, yet fills it at the same time. Stephanie is finally able to say, "Eliana has brought so much joy back into our lives."

Stephanie and Ryan continue to remember their first daughter by encouraging others to do a random act of kindness in Scarlett's memory. Visit the Facebook page "Be the Sunshine for Scarlett,": www.facebook.com/ bethesunshineforscarlett/?ref=br_rs, to see how Scarlett's Sunshine has spread.

"Scarlett's Sunshine Section" was established at the Peters Township Public Library, McMurray, Pennsylvania, in April 2017 with the purpose of providing assistance to children and their families dealing with loss. The materials and resources are available to anyone in need, and several of the books have been donated in Scarlett's memory by The Still Remembered Project. WQED Pittsburgh also donated Sesame Street kits, "When Families Grieve."

JOURNAL PROMPT

Was there anything specific, such as a ceremony, that you did to honor your infant? What are you planning to do to remember your baby?

CHAPTER 9

MY OWN LOSS
KEVIN AND ART

When I left the hospital without my infant twin sons on that cold day in April so long ago, I was given a keepsake booklet containing imprints of their tiny feet and the only photographs of Kevin and Art, taken minutes after their births. The haunting images of my babies, lying side by side and dressed only in the hospital-issued infant T-shirts, became the only tangible confirmation of a void I would never fill.

For the longest time after, those Polaroid photographs of our babies remained in the memory book, tucked away in a closet next to my aging wedding gown, never very far from the surface.

Each time I took the book out, I was told to put it away because the photos were too sad and too difficult to look at. Advice was often to "move on and forget." No matter how many years went by, nothing could be further from the truth than saying I never thought about the babies I lost.

Instead, I held my sons in my heart, and I never forgot. They were always "carried within me."

Perhaps that was the reason behind the instant connection when I first heard of The Still Remembered Project in Pittsburgh and decided to donate my wedding gown to be made into an Angel Gown for an infant to be buried in. Without a second thought, I instinctively knew that donating my own wedding gown was something I had to do.

Since the organization's inception in 2016, Pittsburgh area hospitals have received hundreds of memory boxes, handmade blankets, keepsake holiday ornaments, garden memorials, and Angel Gowns.

I am encouraged today to know that infant loss is no longer a silent sorrow. The cycle of life continues, yet there are some things you never get over.

"How many children do you have?"

Any mother who has lost an infant always will answer with hesitation. Mother's Day, birthdays, anniversaries of a death or burial, and particular seasons of the year continue to trigger bittersweet memories of a child missing from a family.

For me, the manager of the cemetery where our twins were buried became a source of comfort and support. Her name was Anne and she called me each year at Christmastime. We had moved since our babies were born and now live 100 miles from the cemetery in Altoona. Anne was a compassionate voice on the phone, knowing we couldn't visit the gravesite often, and she acted as a guardian, placing a wreath or flowers and faithfully looking after the grave site of our infants to this day, nearly thirty years after. Anne would call in April to let us know that the spring bulbs planted came up on the day that would have been their birthday.

Years passed until we finally met face to face. Thinking that the long-awaited introduction would be easy, within minutes, we fought back tears. Anne's warm compassion gave me inspiration at a time when I needed it most.

She knew how to offer comfort because she, too, is the mother who suffered the loss of her baby.

When I think back to the photographs of Kevin and Art, I will always remember them side by side, wrapped in one blanket and wearing their hospital T-shirts. I initially worried that giving up my wedding gown might just become another heart-wrenching reminder of the loss that has been carried within me. Yet, seeing the gown transformed into Angel Gowns replaced the bittersweet memories with feelings of gratitude for all those who have offered an outpouring of compassion and support to those in need of comfort.

In May, 2018, a touching remembrance of my twin sons Kevin & Art Cantrell was created by Army Veteran and artist Aidan Kitching. (Artistic expression is one way that some veterans help combat symptoms of PTSD.) Aidan's custom painting was commissioned through the Still Remembered Project for Mother's Day.

CHAPTER 10

WHAT WE CAN LEARN

Cambron Wright is a United Methodist pastor and writer living in Bowling Green, Kentucky, who shared an essay on his blog reflecting on his grief and healing after his wife suffered a miscarriage.

Giving a husband's and father's perspective, Pastor Wright is candid and honest about the experience of grief, hoping that those who might read his essay will know that they are not alone. He always remembered many years ago being a new chaplain, and one of his very first calls was to baptize an infant who was near death. That event made a profound impact on him, realizing the intense grief of parents who never had the chance to know their baby.

The following was originally posted on his blog during the month of October—Pregnancy and Infant Loss

Awareness Month, in the hopes of opening a discussion on the often unspoken, isolating loss of miscarriage:

LIFE TO DEATH TO LIFE AGAIN: ONE MAN'S JOURNEY THROUGH THE GRIEF OF MISCARRIAGE

If you or your loved one has recently had a miscarriage, then you are probably feeling something like I felt at the time: lost, confused, depressed, and weighed down with a mess of emotions that you don't know what to do with. If you are anything like me, you have been up searching for articles online to tell you what you should be feeling and doing, because you are dreading the silence that awaits you in the rest of your house.

Maybe you have been praying, afraid that no one is listening on the other end. You see, I think stories help us heal. They make us realize we are not alone. I'm a Christian, a pastor, and a man. Because of this, I often want solutions to problems I can't solve, and answers to questions no one has ever figured out.

After my wife's miscarriage, I realized the need to tell some more of my friends, to let them help me. It's a hard thing, because it seems like the more people we tell, the more real it becomes. And if we keep it private, we can make it a secret, unreal thing—a thing we can forget more easily.

I'm sharing this so you might know that whatever you are feeling right now is okay, and to give you some hope that you will not always feel the way you feel right now.

If you are going through a miscarriage, here's some ways I would encourage you to find healing:

- Remember, there is no easy way to get rid of grief. The only way is through.

- I encourage you to find a friend, find a counselor, find a pastor, and tell them what's going on. They will listen. It will help you to heal. If you are a man, I understand that you are bearing the double pain of the loss itself, and the inability to fully understand your wife's loss. Others can help you process what you are feeling. Let them help you do this.

- Resist the quick healing. Healing will take time, longer than you want it to take.

- Be vulnerable with people you trust. Protect your heart. Some people are not helpful, and some people are. When people are harmful, forgive them; they probably have no way to relate with what you are going through.

- Lean into your love—don't run away from your spouse or partner. Support each other. Let each other take turns crying. Let your man cry; he is going to want to feel strong. Let your wife cry long after you have "gotten over it." We all deal with this stuff differently.

- Have grace for yourself. Meaning: eat too much, watch too much TV. Be less productive. Forgive yourself for doing these things. You are facing a real loss, and it is going to affect you in every way.

- Pray. Meaning: be honest with God. Be angry, be depressed, be sad, and bring all those dark emotions to God. He can handle them, and he can guide us to a place of healing. We can do nothing to separate ourselves from his love: if we bring our true selves to him, we can become more aware of his saving presence even in our times of trouble.

If you are supporting a friend who is going through a miscarriage, here is some encouragement and advice for you:

- Do not talk about how common it is to have a miscarriage. It is common to get cancer as well, but that does not seem to be the compassionate response to it. This is a real loss of a real child. Understand that felt reality, even if the child was only a few weeks old. Knowing that thousands of others are experiencing it at that moment does not make it any easier.

- Silence is always better than harmful clichés. Do not say anything about God's will. Do not explain the problem of evil. Do not say God works in mysterious ways. These are things beyond our understanding. They are never helpful and often harmful.

- Listen deeply, and say "I'm so sorry this happened. I love you so much." Repeat.

- Talk about what happened. If you have a friend or family that is experiencing a miscarriage, don't ignore it. Write a note. Make a phone call. Visit them! Bring them a meal. They need you, but they might not be able to communicate that. Take the initiative. Go and listen in whatever way you can. This may be uncomfortable for you, but we need each other.

- Pray with people, when you are with them and when you are not. They need it. (We had friends pray for us immediately when we told them—this was exactly what we needed, and it brought our friendship with them to a new, deeper, and more intimate place).

- Share your story. If you have had a miscarriage, your story can help people. Reach out, write a note, say I've been there. It helps more than you might know.

Reprinted with permission.
https://cambronblog.wordpress.com

RESOURCES

Compassionate Friends

The Compassionate Friends offers friendship, understanding, and hope to families grieving the death of a child at any age from any cause. With more than 600 chapters and more than 25 closed Facebook pages, it remains the largest self-help bereavement support organization in the U.S. Local chapters offer monthly, peer-to-peer support meetings. Often special events for bereaved families such as a Walk to Remember, a butterfly release, or lantern launch are planned to allow the families to celebrate the lives of all the children gone too soon. These local chapters also often publish periodic chapter newsletters, maintain a website, or host a Facebook page. Chapters can be found by going to the chapter locator on the national website and simply inputting your zip code.
www.compassonatefriends.org

The Lullaby Fund

Provides help and comfort to those who tragically lose an infant by financially assisting with funeral costs.
https://www.lullaby fund.com

March of Dimes

Offers resources for those who have lost an infant during pregnancy or during the first days of life. Miscarriage, stillbirth, and other conditions can cause a pregnancy to end before or during birth. Newborn death can be caused by premature birth, birth defects, or other health issues. If you've had any of these experiences, you may be overwhelmed by your feelings of loss. Learning how people grieve and thinking about ways to remember your baby can help ease your pain and get ready to think about the future. Visit Share Your Story®, an online community where families who have lost a baby can talk to and comfort each other. Sharing your family's story may ease your pain and help you heal. Visit UnspokenStories.org or www.marchofdimes.org to find out more.

Marty Tousley, Grief Counselor RN, MS, FT, DCC
Grief Healing Blog:
www.griefhealingblog.com

Now I Lay Me Down to Sleep

To introduce remembrance photography to parents suffering the loss of a baby with a free gift of professional portraiture. NILMDTS offers the gift of healing, hope, and honor to parents experiencing the death of a baby through the overwhelming power of remembrance portraits. Professional-level photographers volunteer their time to conduct an intimate portrait session, capturing the only moments parents spend with their babies. Parents are gifted with delicately retouched heirloom black-and- white portraits free of charge. These priceless images serve as an important step in the healing recovery for bereaved families. NILMDTS remembrance photography validates the existence and presence of these precious babies by honoring their legacy.
www.nowilaymedowntosleep.org

Pittsburgh Bereavement Doulas

Offering support for grieving parents during and following the loss of a pregnancy or an infant. Labor doulas provide immediate support during stillbirth or miscarriage. When parents learn of a life-limiting diagnosis for their unborn child, doulas will also meet prenatally to help create a birth plan. They are skilled in memory making, photography and final disposition options. Pittsburgh Bereavement Doulas help caregivers and parents mourn and celebrate the lives of their children across their spectrum of needs, from assisting with immediate practical decisions to providing ongoing physical and emotional care.
www.pittsburghbereavementdoulas.com

Project Sweet Peas

Project Sweet Peas is a 501(c)3 national non-profit organization coordinated by volunteers, who through personal experience, have become passionate about providing support to families of premature or sick infants, and to those who have been affected by pregnancy and infant loss. Project Sweet Peas acknowledges the importance of parental involvement in caregiving and decision-making in the neonatal intensive care unit (NICU), and seeks to promote family-centered care (FCC) competencies in hospitals nationwide. Care packages, hospital events, peer-to-peer support, financial aid, educational materials, and other Project Sweet Peas services, support the cultural, spiritual, emotional, and financial needs of families as they endure life in the NICU. Project Sweet Peas makes a lifelong commitment to support families experiencing pregnancy and infant loss.
www.projectsweetpeas.com

Scarlett Lillian Pauley Foundation

Established in loving memory of Scarlett Lillian Pauley who passed in her sleep on January 8th, 2017. Scarlett's passing is considered Sudden Unexplained Death in Childhood (SUDC), which is a category of death in children between the ages of 1 and 18 that remains unexplained after a thorough investigation, including an autopsy. Scarlett's family created this foundation to promote awareness of and raise funds to support research into the medical mystery that took her life and support other bereaved families going through the horrible tragedy of child loss.

www.scarlettsfoundation.org

SHARE Pregnancy and Infant Loss Support

National organization serving those whose lives are touched by the tragic death of a baby through pregnancy loss, stillbirth or in the first few months of life. SHARE strives to set a standard of personalized perinatal bereavement care through a lifetime of support, hope and healing—one family at a time.

www.nationalshare.org

National SHARE Office 402 Jackson Street Saint Charles, Missouri 63301-3468 Phone: 800-821-6819 Email: info@nationalshare.org

The Still Remembered Project

The Still Remembered Project provides bereaved parents and families Christian-based support and encouragement for a loss due to miscarriage, stillbirth, or early infant death. Efforts offer hope and healing throughout all stages of the grief journey with a mission of educating local medical and bereavement communities, providing remembrance keepsakes to families, holding awareness events and hosting a monthly peer support group meeting for bereaved mothers.

https://stillremembered.org

The Sudden Unexplained Death in Childhood (SUDC) Foundation

The only organization worldwide whose purpose is to promote awareness, advocate for research, and support those affected by Sudden Unexplained Death in Childhood (SUDC). The SUDC Foundation provides all services at no cost to families.

www.sudc.org

ACKNOWLEDGEMENTS

There are many to thank who believed in and supported the need for this book, beginning with the *Pittsburgh Post-Gazette* for publishing the feature, "Forever in our hearts," that prompted an overwhelming reader response and connected me to the bereaved mothers and fathers who were willing to be interviewed.

https://www.post-gazette.com/opinion/Op-Ed/2017/05/07/The-Next-Page-Even-in-death-one-s-child-is-forever-in-your-heart/stories/201705070019

With the inception of this book project, many individuals came forward with introductions and suggestions to network and become a part of the community of bereaved parents and those who support them. Though not all are not specifically mentioned in this book, the appreciation I have for their insight and information cannot be measured.

Special thanks to graphic designer, Carolyn Trobaugh, for giving so freely of her time and assistance; to Sharon McHale for her encouragement; Lauren McLean for her invaluable resources and direction; and to my very dear friend, Anne Macklin, for her lifelong empathy and loving guardianship of Kevin and Art's resting place.

I am grateful to Lighthouse Point Press for validating the worth of these compelling stories and understanding the relevance of infant death.

Thank you to my husband and father of our five children, Art, who has always been there.

Finally, sincere and heartfelt gratitude to all of the mothers and fathers who have lost infants—those who courageously shared their poignant experiences with the intent to help others, and to those who never had an opportunity to remember their babies.

ABOUT THE AUTHOR

Human interest writer Joann Cantrell is a Pittsburgh native who has worked for newspapers and magazines and as an award-winning freelancer. With a genuine interest in hearing narratives and the desire to write, share, and preserve the stories of people's lives, she presents her third book, *Carried Within Me—*  *Echoes of Infant Loss.* She is the mother of three adult children and twin sons, Kevin Joseph and Arthur George Cantrell, who were born on April 2, 1990, and died shortly after their birth.

If this book has been meaningful to you, share your story or contact the author:
https://wordpress.com/view/joanncantrell.wordpress.com

GRAPHICS

The cover art image is "Angel taking Baby to Heaven" by Lovetta Reyes-Cairo, artist and bereaved mother living in Utah. Her work explores spirituality, healing, balance, beauty and love. To learn more about this image and other of her works, visit: https://www.loveheartsart.com

The image of the angel gown appearing at the beginning of each chapter was designed by Carolyn Trobaugh. This photograph was taken in memory of Baby Ava by Chelsea Johnson.

CPSIA information can be obtained
at www.ICGtesting.com
Printed in the USA
BVHW031850140720
583741BV00001B/120